# DEDICATION

This book is dedicated to the memory of John Pearson (1946-2022),
who showed us how to enjoy the game we call cricket.

John served the club for many years as an umpire, coach, mentor, treasurer,
committee member and simply as someone who encouraged others,
inspiring so many young people with his infectious enthusiasm.

First published in Great Britain in 2022

INSPIRE CREATIVES

61 Bridge Street, Kington, Herefordshire. HR5 3DJ

www.inspirepublishing.co.uk

ISBN 978-1-7396739-1-8

10 9 8 7 6 5 4 3 2 1

First edition

Book design and text setting by Anna Page.

The editors and Rainhill Cricket Club would like to thank the following supporters who have made this project possible:

Andrew Finney

Martin Lowrie

Peter Mercer

Anna Page

# RAINHILL CRICKET CLUB—150TH ANNIVERSARY YEAR

RCC under 9s (B team)
Cup runners-up, Ainsdale Tournament

John Rotheram
**Chairman**

Mike Rotheram
**Club Captain**

Peter Mercer
**President**

RCC under 9s (A team)
Plate runners-up, Ainsdale Tournament

**RCC 1st XI** v Leigh, 31.7.21

**RCC 2nd XI** v Wigan, 17.7.21

**RCC 3rd XI** v Bootle, 29.7.21

**RCC Women's Super 8s** v Wavertree, 9.6.21

**RCC girls under 10s** at Rainhill Cricket Festival, 12.9.21

**RCC Sunday XI** v Bury, 25.7.21

**RCC Last Man Stands team** v Earlestown, 25.8.21

**RCC women and under 18s girls** 13.9.21

**RCC under 11s** v Liverpool, 27.7.21

**RCC under 13s** v Maghull, 22.4.21

**RCC under 15s**, 17.9.21

**RCC under 18s** v Ormskirk, 28.6.21

# MANY THANKS TO THE FOLLOWING SPONSORS AND SUPPORTERS

BLUE MANGO RESTAURANT & TAKEAWAY

HS

kdp architects

Caffè & Co. Specialty Coffee

KARANDA SOLUTIONS

BLACK SWAN TAX ADVISERS

dys appear unlocking the key to learning

PERFORMANCE MIND

wellpolished

best-one The heart of the community

COEUS INSURANCE MANAGEMENT

NORTHERN FENCING LIMITED

everyshotcounts

Hayes Traditional Butchers

D MORGAN

HUYTON & PRESCOT GOLF CLUB 1905

TP Travis Perkins plc

R.D. WILKES Optometrist

# CONTENTS

# INTRODUCTION

## from Andrew Page, General Editor

As a player with Rainhill Cricket Club since 2014, I feel both proud and privileged to be asked to undertake the task of editing a book celebrating the club's 150th anniversary season.

This book is not intended to be a detailed account of everything that happened at Rainhill Cricket Club during 2021, but is more an attempt to capture the mood, the excitement and the atmosphere during our 150th anniversary season. It is intended for players, members, their families and their friends, but it is also written for cricket fans in general and particularly for those who are followers of other clubs in our local area. I hope this book appeals to the many people who appreciate cricket at this level and who will recognise many of the names and venues mentioned.

Rainhill Cricket Club has always been about people and, in that respect, little has changed in a century and a half. While I am essentially telling the story of a season and of the characters central to the various dramas that unfolded during it, in order to set the backdrop and to celebrate the people who played a significant role in the club's past it seemed appropriate to include an introductory chapter on the club's history. This was only achieved through extensive research, personal visits to former players, factual anecdotes and making sense of assorted written records.

It is important to note that each of the "tales" were separately written in conjunction with relevant players and club officials, and were not written with respect to any other contribution. I have encouraged people to speak for themselves and their perspectives may not always be mine. The source material for much of the narrative surrounding the various teams is match reports written during the season for the club's website, which themselves drew on the views of coaches, team captains and even other volunteers such as scorers. Some credit should naturally go to Geoffrey Chaucer, whose famous works provided the inspiration for the approach I have taken to tell our story.

It should be noted that, due to incomplete records, it has only been possible to provide full statistical data for the 1st, 2nd and 3rd teams. In an ideal world I would have liked to treat all teams equally and provide statistics for every team from the 1st XI to the under 9s, but the information I would need is regrettably unavailable.

I offer my sincere thanks to all who have assisted me. Firstly, I would like to thank my fellow editors: my colleague, Kyrstyna Zielińska, and my wife, Anna. Without their help and guidance (not to mention Anna's patience) this book would simply not have been possible. Secondly, I am grateful to Peter Mercer for his work in researching the club's history—a not inconsiderable challenge given the limited original material available and the absence of intact records. I would also like to mention Mike Rotheram, John Rotheram, Joe Crossley, Matt Yorke and the wider committee, which has been unwaveringly supportive of this project from the outset.

Rainhill Cricket Club has a distinguished history stretching back 150 years.

Like most cricket clubs. Rainhill's history includes numerous highs and lows, successes and disappointments. Entering our 150th year, however, it's reasonable to conclude that the club is on an upwards trajectory and, following eight seasons in the LDCC Premier League and with a rapidly growing active membership, is in as healthy a state as it has ever been.

### Early years (1871-1918)

Times have often been difficult for the club, especially in the early years when simply surviving was an achievement.

The original Rainhill Cricket Club was founded in 1871. Little is known about the first ten years of the club's existence, and the earliest extant scorecard is of a home match against South End in 1881.

Eight years later, in February 1889, a meeting was held in the Commercial Hotel to discuss reforming the cricket club. On the agenda was a proposal to return to playing on Strettle's Field (off Warrington Road), which was owned by a Mr Strettle of Ivy Farm. An extract from the recorded minutes of the meeting states: "they formerly had a cricket club which was a success financially, and during the time it was vogue the cricket played by the members was considered first class".

**Rainhill Cricket Club, c1900**

1889 also saw the re-formed club's first annual ball on 13th December. The Prescot Reporter and St Helens Advertiser reported that this was attended by fifty ladies and gentlemen in the National School Rooms, Rainhill. Catering was provided by the Commercial Hotel.

In April 1894, Rainhill Cricket Club and Athletic Grounds Company Limited was registered and the club was still using Strettle's Field as its home. By 1900 photographic images of Rainhill CC's cricket teams were starting to appear, and some of these survive.

The advent of World War One (1914-1918) meant that the cricket team was disbanded. Such were the harsh realities of war that it was reported that "some of the players never returned". In 1919 a press release reported the winding up of the RCC and Athletic Grounds Company Limited in September.

### The inter-war years (1918-1939)

The war did not spell the end of cricket in Rainhill and the demise of the old club resulted in efforts to re-create a cricket club. On 22nd March 1920 Rainhill Recreation Club was established when several sports teams amalgamated, including the cricketers of Rainhill Cricket Club. Mr Peter Wright of Heyes Farm sublet the pasture field off Warrington Road to the club and the old pavilion was moved the short distance to the new ground. It appears the cricket pitch was not immediately in a sufficiently good condition on which to play.

A photograph of the Rainhill team (right), captioned "pre-1920", shows the players at the Old Lane Ground. However, given that no cricket was played between 1914 and the winding up of the old club five years later, it is more likely that the photograph was taken at some point between 1920 and 1922, after which the move to the new ground took place.

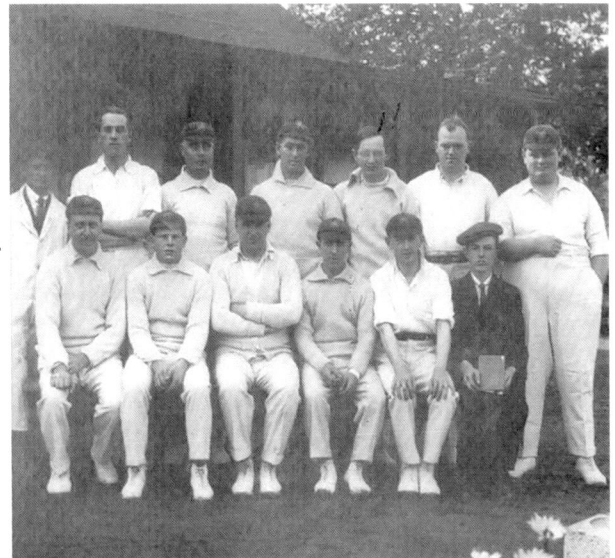

**Rainhill Cricket Club c1920**

Minutes of the club AGM on 22nd March 1922 had a heading of 'Budding cricketers brought to light'. Mention was made of 'Harry Allcock's feat of performing the hat trick against Huyton'. The minutes also outlined details of a ground purchase scheme for the ground on which Rainhill Cricket Club currently plays. "A piece of land 5.75 acres, suitable for all outdoor games, and situated to the east of Victoria Terrace, has been secured at a cost of £479, a deposit of £47.9s 6d having been paid".

Rainhill Recreation Club is believed to have played on the new ground for cricket, tennis, football, hockey, and bowls for the first time in 1923. Photographic images remain of the Recreational Club members enjoying various sports and other activities.

Rainhill became an established club during the 1920s and 1930s, although written records are few and far between.

## Improvements and progression (1939-1970)

In 1952, Ronald Mercer (father of current president Peter Mercer) scored 1000 runs and took 100 wickets in one season. For this phenomenal feat he was awarded a Gunn and Moore bat by the club.

Two years later chairman Peter Houghton purchased a 44' x 20' wooden hut from an airfield in Stretton. The hut was assembled across the old changing rooms. It had a veranda on the front and a scorebox on the side. Houghton's son, Peter Houghton junior (right) was pictured standing in front of the newly acquired structure in 1958. Houghton junior was an excellent bowler for Rainhill and, in 1962, received a trophy from his father for taking 100 wickets in a season

In 1962, further ground improvements saw a septic tank fitted following extensive digging. This was enhanced by a breeze block extension, which provided for the first-time flushing men's and women's toilets. A year later a bar licence was secured and alcohol was provided on the premises for the first time.

In September 1964 local youths set the mainly wooden building structure on fire and the whole building was reduced to rubble. Keith Welsby rang the fire brigade by running down

**Peter Houghton Jr**

Victoria Terrace to use the phone box at the bottom of View Road. At that time there was no phone at the club. The Fire Brigade was unable to access the club via the Victoria Terrace entrance.

At some point prior to the fire the Club Treasurer, Harry Finney (father to current scorer Andrew Finney) had prudently increased the insurance on the building, which provided the monies to build a new clubhouse. Following extensive discussions, it was agreed to clear the old tennis courts and build a large brick clubhouse.

**Rainhill CC 1st XI, late 1960s**

Many of the cricketers supported the project, including Ted Dickin, George Hubbard, Bill Jones, and Frank Davies. Tennis Member Keith Forber led the project and it is suggested that the hardcore for the footings came from a demolished church. Keith Welsby, a Rainhill player in the 1950s, wrote about his experiences at the club, the old wooden structures and the construction of the new clubhouse.

Progress was also taking place on the field. The first team (pictured here in the late 1960s) acquired several promising players on which its future success would be built and, in 1970, the club's second team were Merseyside Cricket Association League Champions.

**Success in the Seventies (1970-1979)**

In 1971 the first team, captained by Frank Davies, were Merseyside Cricket Association League Champions. The second team also continued to make progress under the leadership of captain Jack Williams. Williams was a major character at the club and was team captain for several years (both for the second team and, later, the first) in addition to preparing the wicket for a long period. Unfortunately, the lack of records means that many of his playing achievements cannot be outlined.

In 1975, Dennis Cowley - a long-standing supporter of the club and captain of the second team for many seasons - scored 133 not out for the second team in a home draw.

In 1976, under the captaincy of George Hubbard, the first team were Cheshire Association League Champions. They repeated this success in 1977, when they were also Aggregate Cup winners - a competition for first and second teams. In the same

**Rainhill CC 1st XI, 1978**

year Peter Mercer finished top of the Cheshire Association League batting averages with over 500 runs and a top score of 120 not out. Following Cheshire League success, Rainhill Cricket Club joined the Merseyside Competition in 1978.

In 1979 the ground was used to celebrate the 150th anniversary of the Rainhill locomotive trials. Seating was provided at the top of the ground to watch historic trains passing on the railway line and a gala took place on the main playing area.

## Onwards and upwards (1980-1989)

Rainhill's first team, now captained by Peter Mercer, started the 1980s by finishing as runners-up in the Merseyside Competition Division One. Mercer played for the Merseyside Competition Representative side in the President's Trophy Final defeat at Chester le Street, Durham. Ted Dickin also played a key role with both bat and ball, including an unbeaten 111 at Bromborough Pool.

In 1984 Dennis Cowley scored 700 League runs for the second team including a century (105) and five fifties.

**Ted Dickin**

By 1985 the first team was captained by Peter Woods, who has kindly provided full statistics for the season. Woods scored an unbeaten 107, took 15 catches during the season and was one of four players to score more than 500 runs: Peter Mercer (658), Peter Woods (608), Ted Dickin (590) and George Hubbard (506).

In the following year Ted Dickin and George Hubbard both finished their long-playing careers. They were two quality players and true servants to the club. While full records are unfortunately unavailable to fully outline their achievements, Dickin scored in excess of 500 runs in the 1980, 1984 and 1985 seasons; Hubbard did the same in 1980 and 1982. In the Merseyside Competition, Dickin had a top score of 113 not out and best bowling figures of 8-39 (at Wavertree in 1980); Hubbard's top score was 104.

Peter Mercer continued to score freely and in 1986 amassed 665 runs and took 68 wickets (at an average of 9.11). This was his third consecutive season of achieving in excess of five hundred plus runs and fifty wickets. He took a club record 9-17 and scored a season-best 105 not out. His batting and bowling averages for 1986 were among the best in the first division.

In the same year, Richard Crone scored a fantastic 100 not out for the second team, while Andrew Birkett claimed a hat trick in a 4-14 spell of bowling.

The following year Peter Mercer scored 616 league runs, while Dave Birkett took 64 wickets (at an average of 10.19) with season-best bowling figures of 8-21.

Mercer continued to be the club's leading run scorer into the 1990s and in 1988 hit 577 league runs (also taking 51 wickets at an average of 10.94) including 100 not out in a home victory. In the following season Mercer scored 796 league runs including an unbeaten 131 versus Bromborough Pool. Dave Birkett was the leading wicket-taker in these years, with 63 league wickets in 1988 and 58 in the following year.

1989 saw the retirement of William (Bill) Jones – another player with a long career and for whom full records are not available. A quality batsman with a top score of 93 in the Merseyside Competition, Jones was an excellent wicket keeper who was a big character at the club.

## A time of change (1990-1999)

Peter Mercer and Dave Birkett continued their fine form into the 1990s. Mercer scored 749 league runs, including 122 not out, in 1990 and followed this up in 1991 with an even more impressive 812 runs over the season. This completed ten consecutive seasons of scoring in excess of 500 runs. Birkett took 51 league wickets, at an average of 15.31, in 1990.

Mark Scott took 52 league wickets (at an average of 13.42) for the second team in 1990. In 1991, Andrew Birkett accumulated 587 runs in league competition.

A significant development occurred in 1992 when Ray Ford joined the Rainhill CC as coach and set up the club's first junior section. Ray continued in his role for five years, firmly establishing the junior set-up and producing several successful players. Ray also managed the Competition's Colts team for a period of time.

Ray Ford was also a useful player and in 1993 he scored 505 league runs. In the same season. Dave Marshall scored an unbeaten 100 in a home league victory while Peter Mercer picked up 52 wickets. There was success for the juniors too, with the under 13s winning the Eric Tatlock Cup.

Outstanding junior players included Paul Ford. In 1994 David Bolton and Andrew Ford played for Lancashire CC under 14s and under 11s respectively. In the following year Bolton played for Lancashire's under 15s. 1995 also saw Paul Ford and David Bolton playing for the winning South West Lancashire side in a final at Old Trafford. Paul Ford continued to impress and in 1996 he won the Merseyside Competition Young Player of the Year award with 458 runs.

**Rainhill's Paul Ford and David Bolton lining up for South West Lancashire before a final at Old Trafford**

Jim Fairclough scored a brilliant 1048 runs in the league season for the second team in 1994. The second team won the Norman Cottam Memorial Trophy in 1995. In the 1996 season Steve Toghill scored 623 league runs including a knock of 127 but Andrew Birkett topped the averages with 334 runs at 66.8.

Andrew Ford played for Lancashire under 13s in the 1996 season; in subsequent years he would go on to play for the under 14s and under 15s.

Peter Mercer had his most productive year for the club – in terms of runs scored – in 1997. He scored a total of 846 league runs during the season. In the same year Paul Ford had trials with Lancashire U16s/17s.

In 1998 Richard Green of Lancashire CC played a handful of games for the first team. In spite of this, Rainhill were relegated from Division 1 of the Merseyside Competition. The season saw Ian Blakemore finish his colourful playing career stretching back over 30 years. With his flighted spin he took 289 league wickets, with a best of 8-39 that included a hat trick. He also scored over 1600 runs with a top score of 65 not out.

In 1999 Mike Rotheram, aged just 19, took over as first team captain with an ambition to play in the top division of the Liverpool and District Cricket Competition. Mike scored his first century for the club with 101 not out. In the same year David Birkett finished his 16-year playing career stretching back to 1983. As an opening swing bowler he took 697 league wickets at an impressive average of 13 with best bowling of 8-21.

## New horizons (2000-2009)

John Rotheram became chairman of the cricket club in 2000, taking over from Ian Marshall who had been a longstanding and successful chair. Under Mike Rotheram's captaincy the first team were Division Two champions and Millennium Cup Winners.

Rainhill's progress was aided by Paul Robinson, who had a two-season spell as a professional with the club. His left arm quick bowling and hard-hitting batting style produced several notable performances. Full statistics are not available but in 2001 his top score with the bat was 80 not out and his best bowling figures were 7-20.

Indian professional Vinay Dandekar played for the club at the end of the 2001 season, featuring in seven league games. His most impressive innings was a knock of 113 not out against Liverpool NALGO, which was particularly memorable as his personal contribution amounted for 68.1% of his team's runs.

In 2002 Rehan Rafique from Pakistan became the club's first ever full-season overseas professional. He helped Rainhill win the Kaufman Cup in a final played at Victoria Terrace.

In the following season Rainhill travelled to play St John's from the Isle of Man in the Lancashire Cup and gained a famous victory. After scoring only 133-7 the home side were poised for victory at 132-5. Incredibly, Mattie Dale took 3 wickets and a run out from the last ball to see Rainhill secure victory by one run. The Manx team's last five wickets fell in the space of nine balls.

2003 was a successful year for Rainhill. The second team were once again Norman Cottam Memorial Trophy winners. The first team, managed by Ken Jordan and captained by Mike Rotheram, finished the year as Merseyside and Southport Alliance Champions, Kaufman Cup winners and Lever Cup winners. A league honours list from 2003 underlines just how good a season it was for the club. Rainhill's success was aided by Rehan Rafique's 35 wickets and 980 league runs (at an average of 57.65), which included two centuries. Mike Rotheram contributed an impressive 584 league runs in the season while Mark Kelly took a brilliant 80 league wickets at

**The treble-winning RCC 1st team of 2003**

an average of 10.39. His six five-wicket hauls included best bowling figures of 8-14.

In 2004 James Titmus hit a total of 542 league runs with a best score of 68 not out against Norley Hall. Steve Jordan took 51 league wickets at an average of 15.18. The first team again won the Lever Cup, with Rafique scoring 55 against Moorfield, and reached the final of the Kaufman Cup for the third successive year but were unable to complete the treble. At the end of 2004 Rafique left the club after three successful seasons, having scored over 3000 runs in league and cup cricket. His replacement as overseas professional was Australian Luke Swards, whose fast bowling produced 66 wickets in his first season with a best of 8-64.

Mike Rotheram scored 509 league runs in the 2005 season. Paul Ford scored an unbeaten 158 in a Lancashire Cup win. In the same year Peter Mercer finished his playing career after 30 consecutive years in the first team, scoring over 16000 runs (including seven centuries, all not out) and taking over 800 wickets in league cricket with a top score of 131 not out and best bowling of 9-17.

Ray Ford returned for a second spell in charge of the junior set-up in 2006, and remained coaching until 2011.

In 2006, Bangladeshi Test batsman Mohammad Ashraful was the overseas professional. He did not quite reach the expected heights in the league, scoring 310 runs in 11 games with a best score of 108 not out, but he hit a magnificent 202 in a cup game against Crosby St Mary's in a winning total of 345. Rainhill, now captained by Paul Ford, finished as runners-up in the Merseyside and Southport Alliance and were promoted to the Liverpool and District Cricket Competition (LDCC). They also won the Kaufman Cup, easily beating Whitefield in the final with the help of an Ashraful half century.

2007 was Rainhill's first season in the LDCC Division One - a major achievement for the club but, disappointingly, the season ended in relegation in spite of Mike Rotheram's 597 league runs. Rotheram became the first Rainhill amateur player to achieve the milestone of 500 runs in the LDCC. Overseas player Andrew Ellis, from New Zealand, amassed an impressive 982 runs over the season including a match-winning 167 not out in his first game. He scored two other centuries but, unfortunately, injury limited his bowling to just 31 overs.

**Mike Rotheram**

While the first team suffered relegation in spite of battling performances, the club's under 13s were more successful and, under Ray Ford's leadership, were crowned Merseyside Youth League and Cup Winners. Ryan Williams was selected for Lancashire's under 13s.

In 2008 Rainhill's first team bounced back from the disappointment of demotion and returned to the LDCC Division 1 as winners of the Merseyside and Southport Cricket Alliance. They were helped by overseas professional Khuran Shahzad, from Pakistan, who scored 1,034 league runs (including four centuries) with a top score of 147 not out in a win over Southport Trinity.

2008 was also a successful season for the under 15s, who were Merseyside Youth Divisional Champions and Cup Winners. Ryan Williams was selected to play for Lancashire under 14s.

In 2009 New Zealand Test seam bowler Ian Butler played two games for Rainhill, taking 10 wickets including 7-15 against Maghull. His top score with the bat was 63 in a defeat at Highfield.

Rainhill proved competitive in the LDCC Division One in 2009, finishing eighth. In a successful year for the club the second team finished as champions of the Merseyside and Southport Cricket Alliance Division Two, producing some strong batting performances, including an unbeaten 113 from Matt Dooling in a 10-wicket victory over Rainford. The third team also had a great season, ending the year as 3rd XI (Sunday) 1st Division (East) runners up. Ben Edmundson made his mark for the third team, carrying his bat for an unbeaten 124 against Orrell Red Triangle.

There was more success for the juniors, too. The under 13s nearly pulled off an incredible treble, winning the Merseyside Youth League and Cup and finishing on the losing side in the Lancashire Cup final. The under 15s, captained by Adam Hodgkinson, fared even better, winning the Merseyside Youth League and Cup, the Echo Cup and the Lancashire Cup. The quality of Rainhill's junior players was such that, on the same day, 11 of them represented St Helens District in under 13s or under 15s teams. Ryan Heyes and Ryan Williams played for Lancashire's under 15s.

**Further progress and the Qureshi era (2010-2016)**

Rainhill's first team established themselves in the LDCC Division One, finishing fourth in 2010. Mike Rotherham scored 597 league runs in the season including 105 not out against Sefton Park.  The second team missed out on promotion by ten points, ending the season in third place in the LDCC 2nd XI Division Two. They were aided by the batting of Matt Dooling who scored an unbeaten 129 in a victory over Hightown.  The third team improved on the previous season's second place to finish as league champions.

The biggest change for the club at the beginning of a new decade was the building of a new extension for changing rooms. This was built with funding support from ECB/Football Foundation with Derrick Sparkes leading the project. A new scorebox was also built following a successful funding application by Jonathan Ford for £6,000 to the St Helens Youth Fund.

The following year saw the first team once again finish in fourth place in Division One. Mike Rotheram again scored more than 500 runs over the season and hit his third career century in a home victory over Prestatyn. Mohammad Aslam Qureshi, from Pakistan, joined as our overseas professional. In his first season, bowling left arm spin, Qureshi took 87 league wickets at an average of 11.54 and hit 611 League runs with a top score of 94.

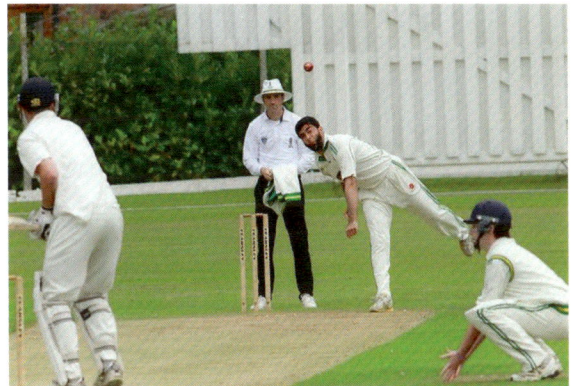

**Mohammad Aslam Qureshi**

In 2012 the first team – for the third successive season – finished fourth in Division One. Mike Rotheram again was the outstanding batsman, recording his top score of the season – 110 – in a win at Alder. Mohammad Aslam Qureshi took 75 league wickets at an average of 9.71.

The second team secured promotion with runners-up in Division Two. The under 20s, captained by Phil Veacock, won the LDCC Bridging Solutions (U20s) T20 Cup.

Qureshi took 106 wickets in 2013 (at an average of 8.98) and scored 506 league runs as the first team finished as runners up in Division One, earning promotion to the LDCC Premier League – the pinnacle of local league cricket. Paul Ford scored his third century for the club with 101 in a win over St Helens Town, while David Atkinson made his maiden first team hundred with an unbeaten 104 in defeat at Orrell Red Triangle.

In their first season in the Premier League, Rainhill's first team finished in a credible ninth place. Mohammad Aslam Qureshi took 94 wickets at an average of 8.30. The second team finished ninth in the 2nd XI Division One; Rob McKeown hit his first century for them with an unbeaten 127 in a drawn match at Lytham. James Clarke was selected for Lancashire's under 11s.

In 2015 the first team were again competitive in the Premier League, finishing seventh. Once more Qureshi was the star bowler and his spin took 97 league wickets at an average of 9.42 – including 9-80 in a win over Bootle.

The following year proved to be Qureshi's last with Rainhill. After helping the first team to an eighth place finish in the Premier League with 79 wickets, he left after six fabulous seasons. Fondly known as 'Mac', he took a remarkable total of 538 wickets in the league with 67 five wickets hauls. His wickets came at an average of 9.80 with an economy rate of 2.00 runs per over. Mac also scored 2497 league runs with a top score of 94.

2016 also saw long-serving wicketkeeper Simon Brown move from the club. He had formed a highly successful partnership with 'Mac.' Also a very useful batsman, Brown's top score of the season was a match winning 83 against Colwyn Bay. In his time with Rainhill, Brown scored in excess of 500 league runs on three seasons: 1994, 2009 and 2013. After four seasons with St Helens Town, Brown returned to Rainhill in 2021.

**Simon Brown**

The second team had a mixed season and finished in eighth place. The outstanding match of the year was a victory over Northop Hall in which Phil Veacock scored 105 in Rainhill's total of 163 before the visitors were bowled out for 82.

**New challenges (2017-present)**

While Qureshi's departure was a blow for Rainhill, the first team (pictured here) responded well to the setback and had their best ever season. Captained by Ben Edmundson, Rainhill finished in third place in the Premier League thanks to performances that showed the depth of talent in the squad. Ross Higham hit a 91-ball hundred against Ainsdale in April, Tyler McGladdery hit a century versus Wallasey in May and David Atkinson scored his second first team century with 105 in a September victory over New Brighton. Three different amateur players scoring centuries in the same season was a first for Rainhill - and it was almost four. Sam Kershaw, who scored 688 league runs, made a knock of 94 versus Southport and Birkdale. The new overseas player, Indian spinner Akshay Arun Darekar, took 89 wickets at an average of 10.83 with best bowling figures of 8-17.

**Tyler McGladdery**

As the leading run scorer in the league with 916 runs at an average of 48.21 (including seven 50s and two centuries), Tyler McGladdery won the Liverpool Competition Player of the Year award. McGladdery's 143 against Wallasey was - and remains - the highest score by a Rainhill player in the Premier League. In all games he scored an incredible 1291 runs.

Akshay Darekar returned for 2018, a season in which the first team finished sixth in the Premier League. He missed a few games but still was able to take 55 wickets with best figures of 7-27 against New Brighton. Tyler McGladdery continued to impress with the bat. His 936 league runs at an average of 49.26 (1,455 runs in all matches) earned him a debut appearance for Lancashire 2nds against Scotland in which he top-scored for Lancashire. Unfortunately for Rainhill, McGladdery's prolific run scoring resulted in him signing for Ormskirk CC for the 2019 season.

The under 15s, now managed by Matt Pennington, were league winners.

2019 saw Qaiser Ashraf join the club as overseas professional. Ashraf took 62 wickets, with a best performance of 7-22, as the first team finished the league season in eighth place. Rainhill were also helped by professionals Luke Procter (Northamptonshire) and Anuj Dal (Derbyshire), who played several games and produced match winning performances.

Paul Duffy took over management of the under 15s from Matt Pennington and helped the team defend their league title. The under 15s also reached the Echo Cup final. Batting first, Rainhill had taken their score to 125-1 before rain intervened. The final was due to be replayed early in the 2020 season but, due to the Covid-19 pandemic, was cancelled.

In the same year, Rainhill CC delivered the ECB All Stars programme, for 5-8 year olds, for the first time. This proved popular with the local community and attracted over 60 participants to one session. Women's and girls' cricket was also introduced by club captain Mike Rotheram.

2020 was a season heavily disrupted by the Covid-19 pandemic. However, a reduced cricket season was possible and, in many respects, was a successful one for Rainhill.

Left arm medium pacer Jamie Harrison (ex-Durham CC) joined the club as a player and junior coach. With the league season replaced with a series of smaller group competitions, the first team emerged as LDCC Love Lane Group D winners. Due to pandemic-related restrictions, the club played without an overseas professional.

Rainhill's 'Last Man Stands' midweek team, captained by Jack Lowrie, finished the season as Warrington and District Champions. The girls' team, only formed a year previously, reached the final of the LDCC Softball Tournament. An ECB grant of £10,000 was obtained by Mike Rotheram to further increase the development of girls' and women's cricket within the club.

In 2021—the club's 150th anniversary season—a full cricket season was possible and relative 'normality' returned. Off the field, technically gifted volunteers successfully designed and built a bespoke website for the club. John Rotheram continued as chairman (his 21st season in the role) while Andrew Finney marked 50 years of scoring for the first team. Joe Crossley, the club's oldest and longest serving player with over 45 seasons behind him, continued as Sunday team captain. Mike Rotheram started his 26th consecutive season playing first team cricket having already scored over 8500 league runs with 4 hundreds and 41 fifties.

Rainhill did not use the services of an overseas player. Tyler McGladdery returned to the club from Ormskirk. Together with Sam Kershaw and David Atkinson (who had a spell with Formby) the talented trio who helped achieve 3rd place Premier League finish in 2017 were reunited.

McGladdery hit 135 not out in a T20 Cup win from only 68 balls (including 11 sixes and 8 fours), setting a new record for the highest individual score in the LDCC section of the competition. The total of 237-4 was the second highest ever LDCC team total in this competition. McGladdery finished 2021 with 950 in all matches and 694 in league competition, including an unbeaten 120 in an impressive victory over eventual champions Northern. The leading wicket taker was Peter Kelly, who collected 42 victims in the league with best figures of 8-59 away to Formby.

The first team qualified for the Lancashire Cup, recording some fine wins along the way, including an away victory at eventual champions Northern. In the first full season for our women's and girls' teams, Rainhill's under 10s girls went the entire season (13 matches) unbeaten, while Rainhill's women also finished as runners-up in the Women's Softball League. The Last Man Stands team regained their league title. There was success for the juniors too as two under 9s teams entered the Ainsdale tournament and finished as cup and plate runners-up.

# THE PRESIDENT'S TALE

Rainhill Cricket Club had for several years been excitingly looking forward to celebrating its 150th anniversary in the 2021 season.

However, the 2020 season had been badly affected by Covid-19 and, as we moved into the 2021 season, the significant challenges from the pandemic remained large.

The club would like to thank the ECB for providing a very welcome 'return to cricket' grant, which relieved several financial pressures with normal fundraising not being available.

Much of the expectation and planning for the anniversary year had to be curtailed around the back drop of community safety with potential financial lose from events not taking place.

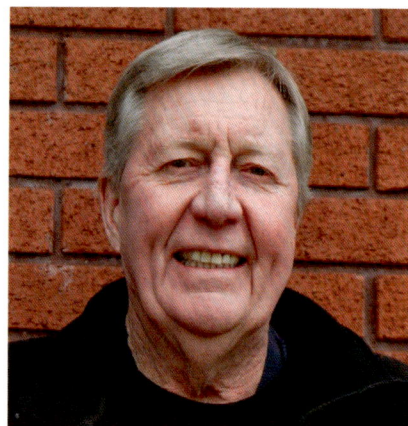

**Peter Mercer**

**Club President**

The Gala on the ground planned for August Bank Holiday Sunday had many stops and starts. Great credit must go to Carlo Albanese and Graham Powell for their drive and inspiration, without which the Gala would not have happened. Excellent weather and super community support resulted in over 700 attendees having a great day. The Club made a higher than expected return on the event and those monies will now be used to provide a new score box / scoreboard.

The anniversary year was also notable for a another major anniversary with Andrew Finney achieving the remarkable milestone of 50 years as a Rainhill CC scorer. Andrew is now amongst a select group of Honorary Life Members.

Myself and Andrew Page complied the history of the Club back to 1871. The production of the history gave me a great opportunity to review my time with the Club since 1975 and look how far we have come as a club in 150 years.

Much of the significant progress that has been made over the last few decades must go to the enthusiasm and ambition of Chair John Rotheram and Club Captain Mike Rotheram.

The club is bigger and better without a doubt with more members than ever before and growing. Since 2014 the first team have played in the Premier League of the Liverpool and District Cricket Competition, regarded as the highest standard regionally. Women's cricket really took off in 2021 and has helped to further increase our member base. The club has a very healthy junior section with boys and girls cricket and we also provided the ECB All Stars and Dynamos cricket sessions during the summer. As we finished off 2021 we agreed to create a new fourth team playing league cricket in the Liverpool and District Cricket Competition, with a Sunday team concentrating on purely recreational matches under the name of Rainhill Recreationals.

The diversity of the players and the increased involvement of parents has positively changed the culture and atmosphere of the club. We also continue to be very thankful for the enthusiastic support of our volunteers.

Without doubt, we have challenges as we move forward but are well placed to continue to prosper both on and off the field.

# THE CHAIRMAN'S TALE

**Chairman John Rotheram (right) takes in a match with Richard Appleton**

I didn't have the best of years health wise but I have enjoyed going to the games. I've been to every 1st team match this season and it's been great to be part of it.

I've been involved with Rainhill CC for over 30 years. I came into it through the football. There were some issues with the Recreation Club back then and I had to sort them out for the benefit of the club. I suppose it's fair to say I did the job I had to. After then, it was a question of me looking after the bar and from that I increasingly became involved with the cricket side.

I took a couple of the junior teams initially, and as Mike was starting to produce the goods in the 1st team I followed him all over the place. It was enjoyable but at that stage I didn't feel that the club was as good as it could have been. When Ian Marshall left as chairman I stepped forward to replace him.

I used to captain the midweek team, which is basically what the LMS team is today. It was also at this time I met John Pearson and appreciated what a great coach he was. I was involved with the junior set-up, and John would just appear and really make it for some of the young people. Not everyone was a good cricketer, but John made them feel as if they were.

Back in 2000 we were struggling to get two teams out at times – you couldn't say that now! It's tremendous to see how much the club has moved on since then, and that is down to the efforts of so many gifted people. The anniversary season was important for the club, especially the Gala which was reminiscent of some of the big galas I organised for the Recreational Club in the 1990s. However, for me what is most special is getting teams out, looking after the club and making sure the club is here for future generations to enjoy.

# THE CLUB CAPTAIN'S TALE

Our anniversary season was a celebration – a celebration of how far Rainhill Cricket Club has come.

You can see that in the number of teams we now have. We cater for all juniors from under 9s to under 18s. We have a developing women and girls' section and we now have eight—eight!—senior teams. We have a truly diverse offering of cricket for all ages and standards, for boys and girls, for people who like the shorter form of cricket and for those who enjoy longer matches. There's a bit there for everyone. We'd like to be even more diverse than we are, but to get to our 150th year and for the club to be in such a healthy state is tremendous.

It's not always been like that. I remember playing for the 1st XI and going to Prestatyn with ten players because we couldn't raise a full team. Sometimes we struggled to put out two teams every weekend—it's fair to say we're a very different club today.

Speaking personally, the highlight of the season was the progress the women's and girls' teams continue to make. As a club we started talking

**Mike Rotheram, Club Captain**

about women's cricket ten years ago but it was a struggle to get going. To now have three teams – under 10s, under 18s and an open age team – is just brilliant. To see them performing so well has been an absolute joy, and I'm sure things will get even better for them.

I was also very proud that the 1st Team remains a force in the Premier League. When I became 1st team captain I had a target of reaching the Premier League by 2005—we eventually achieved that but not until 2014!  Since then we've done well to establish ourselves and Lancashire Cup qualification was a fitting reward for some excellent performances in 2021.

However, Rainhill CC is about so much more than the 1st team. We're about providing something for everyone: aspiring juniors, casual players, people who want to play at the very highest level, women, people who perhaps have never even played before. They're all welcome here and that's absolutely the way it should be.

There's a real family feel about the club and we've never had so many young people involved. The Gala was utterly brilliant and was a great way of connecting with our local community.

Successful clubs need people who are passionate about the club and it's been encouraging to see more of them becoming involved with our cricketing family. Hopefully in the coming years we can grow it even more!

**Rainhill 1st XI v Leigh (a), 31.7.21**

*Back row: Andrew Finney (scorer), Mike Rotheram, Ross Higham, Ben Edmundson (c),
David Atkinson, Peter Kelly, Tyler McGladdery
Front row: Jack Lowrie, Liam O'Toole, Rob McKeown, Luis Duffy, Sam Kershaw*

The 1st team's season was preceded by three friendly matches against Liverpool, Widnes and Birkenhead Park respectively. Rainhill finished on the losing side in each of the matches, although an unbeaten half century from Ross Higham against Liverpool and a contribution of 58 from James Clarke at Widnes provided reasons to feel positively about Rainhill's batting capabilities.

The league season began away to **Orrell Red Triangle**. Batting first, Orrell made a modest 152 as Peter Kelly (4-45) and Jack Lowrie (2-36) created problems for the home team throughout the innings. Dominic Hayes, batting at number 9, offered some stoic defiance with an unbeaten 31 but Rainhill were pleased with their work in the field and chased down the moderate target with relative ease. Tyler McGladdery (83) and James Clarke (44) shared a partnership of 148 before Cameron Sharp took two late wickets for Orrell.

**James Clarke in action v Orrell**

Following the eight-wicket victory at Orrell, Rainhill recorded an even more impressive win over **Wigan** at Victoria Terrace. In a terrific all-round team performance, Rainhill emerged victorious in the first home match of the anniversary season by a margin of 130 runs. Batting first, Tyler McGladdery hit a second successive half century in an innings of 78, while Sam Kershaw added an unbeaten 68 as Rainhill posted 222-3. James Clarke batted well but, as in the Orrell match, fell just short of what would have been a deserved half-century. In response, Wigan struggled against the precision of Rainhill pace bowlers Jamie Harrison (3-5) and Liam O'Toole (3-43). Only wicketkeeper Patrick Howley offered any meaningful resistance, hitting 40 from 27 balls before he was caught by McGladdery off the bowling of spinner Peter Kelly (3-19). The visitors were all out for 92 and Rainhill's season was off to the perfect start.

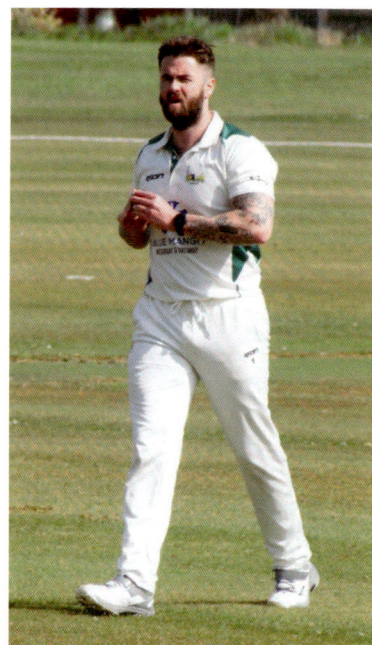

**Jamie Harrison**

Rainhill's next two matches, against **Sefton Park** and **Leigh**, were rained off. The following match, a home fixture against **Wallasey**, saw Rainhill brought back down to earth with a jolt. Buoyed by two comfortable wins Rainhill went into the match with justifiable confidence; however, Wallasey – with overseas professional Sunit Ruikar in their line-up – scythed through Rainhill's top order with Ruikar finishing with barely believable figures of 8-26. James Clarke top scored with a creditable 27 as the home side were dismissed for 66. Jack Lowrie and Liam O'Toole took a wicket apiece to dismiss Wallasey's openers, but the visitors reached their target in just 13.4 overs.

**Tyler McGladdery in T20 action**

Following this setback, the 1st XI travelled to **Maghull** for a Thursday evening T20 match in the ECB Club T20 Cup. An unbeaten 135 from 68 balls for Tyler McGladdery put Rainhill in a strong position and he was supported by captain Ben Edmundson (42) and Sam Kershaw (32) as Rainhill posted an impressive total of 237. McGladdery's knock was the highest individual score ever recorded in the LDCC's section of the T20 Club competition. The previous record belonged to Leigh's Tom Foster who hit 118 in 64 balls against Highfield in 2018.

The target was too much for Maghull who tried to make a game of it but were pegged back by Jamie Harrison, who took 4-15. Joe Campbell (29 not out) and Mohammad Nazaz (20 not out) helped the home side recover from 44 for 6 to post a total of 90 for 6 from their 20 overs, but the result was never in doubt and Rainhill progressed to the next round of the competition.

The next challenge for Rainhill was a visit to **Formby**. In what was to prove one of the most extraordinary games of the season, the home side won the toss and elected to bat first. Formby moved onto 79 for 1 before Rainhill's captain, Ben Edmundson, introduced spinner Peter Kelly into the attack. It was an inspired decision as Kelly turned in arguably one of his best ever performances to take 8 wickets for 59 runs. Formby were able to move on to 212-9 but, given the pitch and the conditions, Rainhill were confident in their ability to chase down the required total.

Rainhill's innings started positively and, at 91 for 2 with the in-form Tyler McGladdery and David Atkinson in the middle, the match seemed to be going according to Rainhill's plan. However,

Formby introduced their own spinners, Jackson Darkes-Sutcliffe and Saad Humayan, who spectacularly turned the game around. Darkes-Sutcliffe struck first to remove Atkinson for 32, a wicket that signalled the beginning of a stunning batting collapse. Formby's spinners took eight wickets for just 10 runs as Rainhill inexplicably and meekly surrendered, falling to a 111-run defeat. It was a difficult outcome to take given Kelly's inspired bowling and the fact that, until the final eight overs, Rainhill had not looked in any difficulty at all.

**Rainhill celebrate as Peter Kelly takes eight wickets at Formby**

On the following Saturday Rainhill hosted **Bootle**. Seeking to bounce back from defeat, Rainhill batted first and positive contributions from David Atkinson (41), Sam Kershaw (29) and Mike Rotheram (29) helped amass a competitive total of 190-8. It was a target that Bootle never realistically looked capable of chasing and Rainhill reduced the visitors to 94-6 before Scott Butterworth and Toby

**David Atkinson**

Lester came together to bat out for the draw. While disappointed not to have secured the win, Rainhill were satisfied with the way they approached the game following the collapse at Formby.

Rainhill's next match was a tricky game away at unbeaten league leaders **Northern**. Batting first, Northern posted 240-3 with Liam Grey (63), Chris Laker (61) and Andrew Clarke (73 not out) all recording half-centuries. Peter Kelly took 2-76 but Northern had posted a target that would be difficult to chase down. Rainhill, however, were not overawed and – led by opener Tyler McGladdery – played with determination and resilience.

The visitors were pegged back by former Rainhill bowler Tomas Sephton (5-109) and, when Mike Rotheram was out without scoring, Rainhill were on 117-4. However, McGladdery was still at the crease and, aided by David Atkinson (31) and Ben Edmundson (27), Rainhill moved ever closer to the target. When Sephton struck to dismiss the Rainhill captain, the visitors were on 225-6 and the game was on a knife-edge. Things became more tense when Jamie Harrison (7) and Peter Kelly (0) were out quickly, leaving Rainhill needing to find four runs and Northern just two wickets for victory.

It was McGladdery, fittingly, who had the final say with a perfectly timed stroke to the boundary. He finished on an unbeaten 120, but it was the nature of the knock that proved significant in the context of the match. The runaway leaders had been derailed by a remarkable innings characterised by defiance and fluency. After the match, Club Captain Mike Rotheram said of McGladdery's innings; "It was the best knock I have seen from any Rainhill player in the 27 years I have been playing at the club. Tyler is the best amateur player I have ever seen and deserves to be playing professional cricket."

**Tyler McGladdery**

After the drama at Northern, Rainhill faced **Colwyn Bay** in a midweek ECB Club T20 Cup match. Without McGladdery, Rainhill's batsmen posted a moderate 133 for 5 from 20 overs with Sam Kershaw, Ben Edmundson, Mike Rotheram and Jamie Harrison all scoring over 25. They would have hoped to have posted something more competitive, but fortunately Rainhill's bowlers restricted Colwyn Bay's opportunities and the Welshmen were all out for 76 from 16.4 overs. Jack Lowrie took 3-16 as Rainhill progressed to the quarter-finals.

A trip to **New Brighton** came next for Rainhill. An eight wicket victory helped move them to fifth in the Premier League as Sam Kershaw (53 not out) and Mike Rotheram (44) helped Rainhill successfully reach a target of 182. Former Lancashire all-rounder Luke Procter had previously pitched in with 5-47 while Jamie Harrison took a well-deserved 4-48.

Procter also helped inspire another relatively straightforward win the following week, this time at home against strugglers **Southport and Birkdale**. Rainhill batted first, with Procter hitting an unbeaten 61 and Tyler McGladdery contributing 71

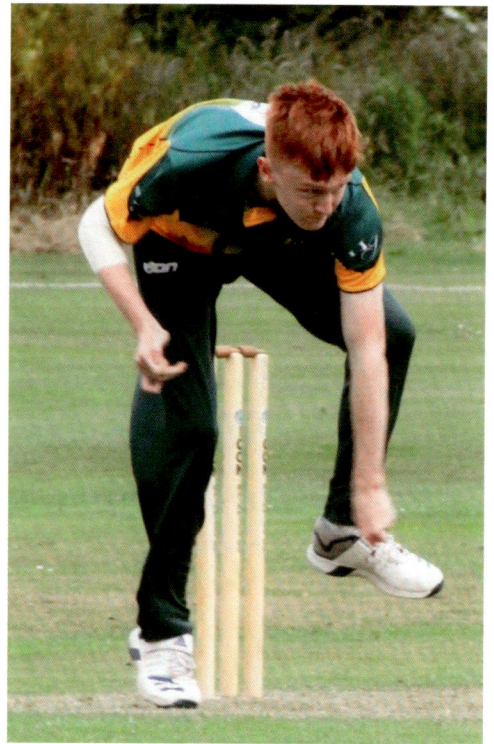
Jack Lowrie

runs as the home side declared on 222-5. In reply, Southport and Birkdale were all out for 93. Procter finished with figures of 4-20 while Jack Lowrie showed his value as a key attack bowler, chipping in with 3-29. The 130-run win moved Rainhill into third place in the league.

Luke Procter

The following day Rainhill hosted **Leigh** in the ECB Club T20 Cup quarter-finals. In a thrilling encounter, watched by around 200 spectators, Rainhill batted first and made an excellent 195-8, with Sam Kershaw (55) and Tyler McGladdery (50) posting half-centuries. Unfortunately for Rainhill, Leigh proved more than equal to the challenge and former Lancashire batsman Karl Brown (71), supported by Sam Dorsey (90 not out), led Leigh to victory with three balls to spare in spite of two wickets for David Atkinson (2-23).

With the T20 Cup adventure at an end, Rainhill's next match was at **Ormskirk**. Aided by Tyler McGladdery, who made an impressive 80 despite a soggy outfield, and an unbeaten 60 from David Atkinson, the visitors posted a competitive total of 220-5 declared. Rainhill had worked themselves into a strong position and Liam O'Toole made an early breakthrough when he trapped Alex Rankin lbw for 3. However, an incredible partnership between Robert Rankin (107 not out) and Taylor Cornall (96 not out) steered Ormskirk to victory.

Rainhill's next opponents were **Orrell Red Triangle**, who they had comfortably beaten on the opening day of the season. Orrell looked stronger

Sam Kershaw

on their visit to Victoria Terrace and Ammer Mirza (44) and Sam Heely (39) offered not only defiance but some positive shots as they helped their side to 187-7. Peter Kelly took 4-62 for Rainhill, who were optimistic of reaching the target set for them before the weather intervened. With the home side having reached 13-1, heavy rain meant that no further play was possible and both teams had to make do with five points each.

**Peter Kelly**

Next up for Rainhill was a meeting with **Wallasey** in the Ray Digman Trophy, a 20-overs competition. The match was a lot closer than the previous encounter between the teams. Wallasey batted first and, largely thanks to a superb half-century from Jamie Crawley, closed their innings on 119-5. Rainhill bowled well to reduce Wallasey's opportunities and captain Ben Edmundson took three wickets. Rainhill made heavy weather of the run chase and, while Tyler McGladdery (35) and Edmundson (24) made positive contributions, fell just four runs short of their target.

Rainhill returned to league action as they travelled to **Wigan**. Peter Kelly once again was outstanding with the ball, as his spin bamboozled Wigan's batsmen and earned him figures of 7-18. All out for 74, Wigan refused to throw in the towel and Vinay

**Liam O'Toole**

Choudhary took 3-31 to give the visitors a scare. However, Tyler McGladdery (46 not out) and Rob McKeown (11 not out) weathered the storm and helped Rainhill across the finish line.

The Wigan victory had moved Rainhill into second place in the Premier League and there was a growing belief that the 150th anniversary season could be memorable for all the right reasons. Success at Wigan was followed by a 4-wicket home victory over bottom side **Sefton Park** in which a masterclass in pace bowling from Jack Lowrie (4-26) wore down and bowled out Rainhill's stubbornly defiant opponents. Lowrie was supported by Liam O'Toole (4-33) as Sefton Park were dismissed for 144. Despite a few setbacks Rainhill eventually ran out comfortable winners, with Ben Edmundson hitting 37 in the successful pursuit.

The next fixture was the much-anticipated clash between Rainhill and **Leigh**, placed second and third in the Premier League. Eager to avenge the T20 Club Cup defeat a few weeks earlier, Rainhill batted first and posted 179. A half-century from Sam Kershaw and a useful knock of 40 from Ross Higham meant that Leigh were presented with a competitive, if not exactly daunting, target. Leigh got off to the worst start in their innings when opener and captain Paul Farrar was bowled by Liam O'Toole for 1, but the home team recovered and moved onto 45 without further loss.

At this point Ben Edmundson brought Peter Kelly and David Atkinson into the attack. The spin duo shared nine wickets as they bowled with deadly accuracy, backed up by some outstanding work in the field. Atkinson (5-30) and Kelly (4-59) had made a good team look distinctly ordinary as Rainhill cemented their position in second place.

Rainhill's next match was also away – this time at **Southport and Birkdale**. Tyler McGladdery struck another half century as Rainhill declared on 200-5 and Liam O'Toole took an early wicket to dent the home team's hopes, but heavy rain caused the abandonment of a match Rainhill had looked destined to win.

Rainhill's hopes of a top-three finish were dealt a further blow when they were beaten at home by **Ormskirk**. Rainhill struggled to 152 with Liam O'Toole top-scoring with an unbeaten 35, but had no answer to Ormskirk's opening batsman Gary Knight. Captain Knight struck 103 from just 65 – including 5 sixes – as Ormskirk eased to the double over Rainhill. It was a game to forget for the home side, who looked to immediately bounce back against **New Brighton** the following week.

**Mike Rotheram**

Unfortunately the weather had other ideas and no play was possible in that match. The next visitors to Victoria Terrace were **Formby**, who had been involved in a gripping encounter with Rainhill earlier in the season. There was once again plenty of action as a half-century from Mike Rotheram and a useful 41 from Rob McKeown helped Rainhill to 193-7 declared. Formby were apparently cruising towards victory on 147-1 before Rainhill's spinners almost pulled off an incredible victory. Firstly, Mike Rotheram took a fine catch off Peter Kelly's bowling to dismiss James Seward for 64. Formby then recovered and moved their score onto 175 before a flurry of wickets reduced them to 190-8. Everything was set for the tense finale but it was Formby who held their nerve and scraped home, leaving Rainhill to rue missed opportunities. James Clarke (4-14) and Peter Kelly (3-51) had performed heroically in the circumstances but plaudits were no substitute for points at the business end of the season.

In the following match, a home fixture against **Northern**, the league leaders gained revenge for the earlier defeat with a 111-run victory. Jack Lowrie took 3-46 and reduced Northern to 21-4, but the visitors were able to recover and close their innings on 220-6. Northern's Andrew Clarke made a superb 122 while Justin Snow hit a patient 59.

**Jack Lowrie**

Rainhill got off to a dismal start from which they never really recovered. Ross Higham (40) and Sam Kershaw (20) at least offered some resistance, but the run chase never realistically looked on. The comprehensive nature of the defeat was particularly disappointing.

Rainhill went into their last two games knowing that a win in either would be enough to assure a top five league finish and qualification for the 2022 Lancashire Cup. Both matches were played away, the first at **Wallasey** who recorded a 97-run win in spite of some excellent bowling from David Atkinson (4-84). Rainhill were never at the races and, chasing 224, slumped to 126 all out. Mike Rotheram top-scored with 33 as he sought to engineer a late fightback but it was too little, too late.

The final match of the season, at **Bootle**, took on particular significance as the home side were seeking to avoid relegation while Rainhill were seeking to qualify for the Lancashire Cup. Rainhill recovered from early setbacks and were eventually all out for 189, with Ross Higham's outstanding knock of 86 giving the visitors something to bowl at. Unfortunately Rainhill's depleted bowling attack was unable to ask any real questions of Bootle's openers, Will Hale and former

England batsman Owais Shah. A brilliant performance from Hale (90 not out) and Shah (88 not out) guided Bootle to a ten-wicket victory which was, in the final analysis, utterly irrelevant: Southport convincingly beat Leigh meaning the batting heroics at Wadham Road were in vain and Bootle were relegated for the first time in their 188-year history.

It looked as if Rainhill had missed out on a top five place and would therefore not take part in the following season's Lancashire Cup. However, as Ormskirk won the cup outright a few days later and would therefore defend their title as champions, Rainhill took the additional LDCC place in the competition.

It had been a disappointing end to a promising league campaign, but Lancashire Cup qualification seemed just reward for Rainhill's performances before those final six matches. The 1st team showed they are capable of beating the very best and were at times unlucky, especially with matches against Sefton Park, Orrell, Southport and New Brighton either cancelled or abandoned due to rain. There are plenty of positives to carry forward and several great games will live long in the memory – and not just the ones Rainhill won!

**Ross Higham**

## LIVERPOOL & DISTRICT CRICKET COMPETITION

### PREMIER LEAGUE

#### Final Standings

| | Pl | w | l | wd | wcn | ld | lcn | d | t | Ab | ND | wc | lc | BatP | BowlP | Pen | Pts |
|---|---|---|---|---|---|---|---|---|---|---|---|---|---|---|---|---|---|
| Northern | 22 | 15 | 3 | 0 | 0 | 0 | 0 | 1 | 0 | 1 | 2 | 0 | 0 | 40 | 36 | 0 | 391 |
| Wallasey | 22 | 13 | 4 | 0 | 0 | 0 | 0 | 2 | 0 | 2 | 1 | 0 | 0 | 46 | 35 | 0 | 356 |
| Leigh | 22 | 12 | 5 | 0 | 0 | 0 | 0 | 1 | 0 | 2 | 2 | 0 | 0 | 31 | 25 | 0 | 316 |
| Ormskirk | 22 | 10 | 7 | 0 | 0 | 0 | 0 | 0 | 0 | 3 | 2 | 0 | 0 | 32 | 28 | 0 | 285 |
| Formby | 22 | 9 | 6 | 0 | 0 | 0 | 0 | 3 | 0 | 1 | 3 | 0 | 0 | 33 | 35 | 0 | 268 |
| **Rainhill** | **22** | **8** | **8** | **0** | **0** | **0** | **0** | **1** | **0** | **3** | **2** | **0** | **0** | **33** | **33** | **0** | **251** |
| Wigan | 22 | 7 | 11 | 0 | 0 | 0 | 0 | 0 | 0 | 3 | 1 | 0 | 0 | 27 | 41 | 0 | 228 |
| Orrell RT | 22 | 7 | 8 | 0 | 0 | 0 | 0 | 1 | 0 | 3 | 3 | 0 | 0 | 20 | 37 | 0 | 227 |
| New Brighton | 22 | 7 | 12 | 0 | 0 | 0 | 0 | 0 | 0 | 3 | 0 | 0 | 0 | 30 | 40 | 0 | 225 |
| Southport | 22 | 5 | 11 | 0 | 0 | 0 | 0 | 4 | 0 | 0 | 2 | 0 | 0 | 43 | 47 | 0 | 200 |
| Bootle | 22 | 5 | 8 | 0 | 0 | 0 | 0 | 4 | 0 | 4 | 1 | 0 | 0 | 26 | 49 | 0 | 200 |
| Sefton Park | 22 | 1 | 16 | 0 | 0 | 0 | 0 | 1 | 0 | 3 | 1 | 0 | 0 | 24 | 52 | 0 | 116 |

# FIRST TEAM STATISTICS 2021

## League and Cup matches only

# BATTING

(minimum qualification: 3 innings)

| | Games | Inns | Not Outs | Runs | Top Score | Ave | 50s | 100s | Strike Rate |
|---|---|---|---|---|---|---|---|---|---|
| Tyler McGladdery | 24 | 21 | 4 | 914 | 135 | 53.8 | 6 | 2 | 77.9 |
| Sam Kershaw | 26 | 23 | 4 | 527 | 68 | 27.7 | 4 | 0 | 66.9 |
| Ross Higham | 24 | 18 | 3 | 340 | 86 | 22.7 | 1 | 0 | 72.2 |
| David Atkinson | 24 | 20 | 2 | 314 | 60 | 17.4 | 1 | 0 | 85.3 |
| Mike Rotheram | 22 | 17 | 2 | 312 | 51 | 20.8 | 1 | 0 | 44.6 |
| Ben Edmundson | 25 | 17 | 3 | 281 | 42 | 20.1 | 0 | 0 | 76.6 |
| James Clarke | 22 | 19 | 0 | 260 | 44 | 13.7 | 0 | 0 | 43.0 |
| Rob McKeown | 12 | 10 | 2 | 137 | 41 | 17.1 | 0 | 0 | 56.4 |
| Luke Procter | 4 | 3 | 2 | 123 | 61 | 123 | 1 | 0 | 117.1 |
| Liam O'Toole | 21 | 11 | 5 | 95 | 35 | 15.8 | 0 | 0 | 73.1 |
| Jamie Harrison | 13 | 6 | 2 | 64 | 29 | 16.0 | 0 | 0 | 115.2 |
| Simon Brown | 15 | 9 | 3 | 56 | 21 | 9.3 | 0 | 0 | 28.1 |
| Jack Lowrie | 25 | 8 | 2 | 14 | 8 | 2.3 | 0 | 0 | 37.8 |
| Peter Kelly | 24 | 8 | 5 | 7 | 5 | 2.3 | 0 | 0 | 14.3 |

# BOWLING

(minimum qualification: 20 overs)

| | Overs | Maidens | Runs | Wickets | Best Bowling | 5-wicket Haul | Econ Rate | Strike Rate | Ave |
|---|---|---|---|---|---|---|---|---|---|
| Peter Kelly | 228.3 | 30 | 828 | 42 | 8-59 | 2 | 3.62 | 32.6 | 19.71 |
| David Atkinson | 126.2 | 11 | 501 | 19 | 5-30 | 1 | 3.97 | 39.9 | 26.37 |
| Jamie Harrison | 103.3 | 13 | 377 | 18 | 4-15 | 0 | 3.64 | 34.5 | 20.94 |
| Liam O'Toole | 132.5 | 20 | 478 | 18 | 4-33 | 0 | 3.60 | 44.3 | 29.56 |
| Jack Lowrie | 140.0 | 24 | 542 | 17 | 4-26 | 0 | 3.87 | 49.4 | 31.88 |
| Luke Procter | 35.0 | 7 | 100 | 11 | 5-47 | 1 | 2.86 | 19.1 | 9.09 |
| James Clarke | 26.3 | 0 | 141 | 7 | 4-14 | 0 | 5.32 | 22.7 | 20.14 |
| Ben Edmundson | 54.4 | 4 | 262 | 6 | 3-15 | 0 | 4.79 | 54.7 | 43.67 |

# THE 2ND TEAM'S TALE

**Rainhill 2nd XI v Wigan (h), 17.7.21**

*Back row: David Crossley (scorer), Ollie Powell, Sam Williamson, Owen Groom, Adam Edwards,*
*Mark Viggars (c), David Pennington, Phil Morgan*
*Front row: Jack Ellis, Luis Duffy, Stevie Pennington, Ethan Powell*

The 2nd team's league campaign was preceded by a friendly at **Sutton St Helens**, which they lost by three wickets despite some positive batting from Owen Groom and captain Mark Viggars.

Their opening match of the league season was a tough one at home to **Old Xaverians**. The visitors won the toss and elected to bat but, when David Pennington dismissed both openers, Old Xaverians looked in trouble at 22-2. However, Mark Dilworth (40) and Joseph Staunton (53 not out) led the fightback as their team reached 180-5 from 45 overs.

It wasn't plain sailing for Rainhill's batsmen, but Mark Viggars (69 not out), Luis Duffy (41) and Phil Morgan (36 not out) helped the home side to a well-deserved six-wicket victory.

The perfect start to the season came to a halt at **Wigan** the following week. Batting first, Wigan put on 239 runs for the loss of seven wickets. Despite some disciplined bowling, especially from

**Mark Viggars**

David Pennington (3-67), Wigan's batsmen frequently found the boundary. Jack Maddocks (66) and Ryan Ouwerkerk (59) both hit half centuries at a rate above a run per ball. The target always looked beyond Rainhill and although Liam Yate played a dramatic innings worth 46 – including 10 fours – the visitors were all out for 125.

Rainhill's next two scheduled games – against **Wavertree** and **Highfield** – fell victim to the weather. The enforced break was followed by a five-wicket defeat at **Birkenhead Park**. Rainhill reached 156, thanks to a patient 47 from Owen Groom and an entertaining contribution of 31 from 21 balls by Adam Edwards, batting at number nine. Stand-in captain Simon Brown managed his bowlers effectively as Edwards, David Pennington and Sam Williamson all created problems for Birkenhead Park's batsmen. However, despite taking regular wickets, they were unable to remove Ian Cooper until he had scored 71, by which point the home side were just 16 runs short of victory. Doug Pyrke and Chris Foran helped Birkenhead Park reach their target as Rainhill went down to their second defeat of 2021.

**Liam Yate**

Next up for Rainhill was a home match against **Ainsdale**, where half-centuries from Rob McKeown (69) and Phil Morgan (50) helped the team to a total of 189-8. In reply, Ainsdale got off to a positive start and reached 41 without loss. However, Adam Edwards (2-24) and David Pennington (2-32) regained the upper hand. Although opener Joel Barlow struck a defiant 54, no-one else was able to stay with him as wickets regularly fell. The run chase petered out, as did the contest, and both sides ultimately settled for a draw as Ainsdale's innings closed on 141-6.

**Luis Duffy**

The performance against Ainsdale gave Rainhill reasons for confidence ahead of the trip to **Northop Hall**. Rainhill put the home side in to bat but, in spite of a wicket apiece for Jack Lowrie, David Pennington and Adam Edwards, Northop Hall played positively to reach 183-4. Evan Withe (47) and Archie Sussex (47 not out) helped their team to what appeared a competitive, if not formidable, total.

Rainhill's innings was a real battle as momentum swung one way and then another. Luis Duffy (47), Owen Groom (29) and Mark Viggars (31) all made positive contributions with the bat, but some excellent bowling from Joshua Leach (4-40) saw Rainhill slip from 122-3 to 144-7. In a tense finale, Phil Morgan (15 not out) and Sam Williamson (1 not out) steered the visitors to a two-wicket victory.

The next game, at home to eventual champions **Colwyn Bay**, saw Rainhill skittled out for 125. Luis Duffy top-scored for the home team with 26, but there was not much to cheer about as Colwyn Bay had little difficulty in reaching the modest target set. The league defeat was followed by cup action as Rainhill travelled to **Leigh** for a midweek T20 match in the Tittershill Cup. Leigh reached 182-4 thanks to an unbeaten 92 from Daniel Humphreys and, while Owen Groom (30) and Adam Edwards (20) took a positive approach, the target proved beyond the visitors.

Rainhill faced **Leigh** again a few days later, this time in a league match at Victoria Terrace. Despite a superb unbeaten 69 from 80 balls for Rob McKeown, Rainhill struggled and collapsed to 119 all out. Deepak Gupta (2-29) struck twice to remove openers Rees Abbott and Siddharth Bhattacharyya early but the target was never enough against a strong Leigh side and they reached 123 for the loss of 4 wickets.

Rainhill travelled to **Spring View** in need of a morale-boosting win and that is exactly what they got thanks to a terrific team performance. Bowlers David Pennington (4-36) and Jack Ellis (4-83) helped put Rainhill in a strong position before a ninth-wicket partnership of 56 from just 24 balls

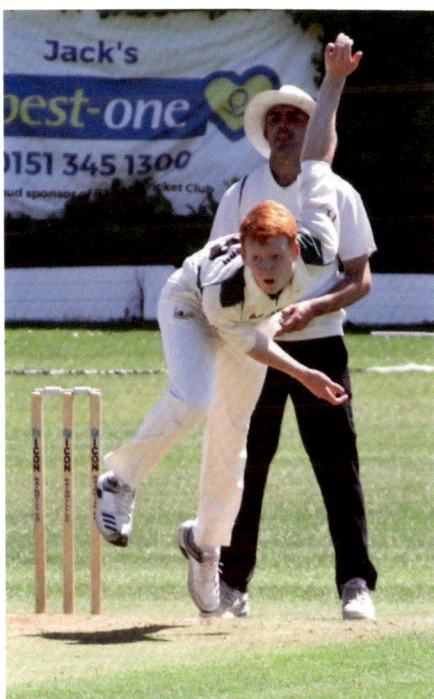

**Rob McKeown**

took Spring View to a total of 205-8. Nathan Barnes' incredible late knock included 5 fours and 5 sixes .

Some teams would have been despondent after conceding 56 runs in the final four overs, but Rainhill were determined. This determination was matched by fluent strokeplay from Luis Duffy

(53) and Rob McKeown (54), with others pitching in with useful contributions as the visitors reached 206-6 in 42.4 overs. It was a fine win that underlined Rainhill's potential and batting strength.

Rainhill's batting abilities were apparent in the next match, at home to neighbours **Rainford**. Put into bat, Rainhill reached 172-9 with Jack Ellis contributing 68 – his best score for the 2nd team. Andrew Harrison impressed for Rainford, taking 6-37, but the total looked a good one on a pitch not offering a great deal for batsmen. Rainford struggled to get going and, although captain Mark Brook held out for a defiant 68, no-one was able to offer him much support as wickets tumbled. After Brook was finally out, caught by Sam Ellis off the bowling of Sam Williamson (3-26), Simon Webster and Josh Spencer held out to secure the draw. It was a disappointing result for Rainhill, but they had every right to feel positive about their performance.

**Sam Williamson**

Another strong performance followed, this time at **Old Xaverians** where Phil Morgan took seven wickets as the

**Owen Groom**

promotion hopefuls were bowled out for 108. Morgan's 7-41 represented his best bowling for Rainhill and was more impressive given that it came against a team unbeaten since the opening day of the season. Faced with a moderate target, Rainhill raced to 69-3 before, cruelly, heavy rain intervened making further play impossible. It was tough on Rainhill, who had put in arguably their best performance of the season and deserved a better outcome. However, the result stretched their unbeaten run to three matches.

The following week Rainhill welcomed **Wigan** to Victoria Terrace and proceeded to give a positive account of themselves in the field. Batting first, Wigan were all out for 135 with Owen Groom, Oliver Powell, Sam Williamson and Jack Ellis each picking up two wickets. Unfortunately, Rainhill were unable to build on this as Adam Samouelle (4-36) and Daniel Yates (2-11) ripped through the top order, reducing the home side to 27-5. Rainhill recovered a little with Phil Morgan pitching in with 17 runs and Sam Williamson contributing an unbeaten 16, but Harry Jackman (4-19) saw off the tail-enders to confirm a 56-run win for Wigan.

The Wigan defeat was difficult to take after recent strong batting performances and Rainhill looked to bounce back immediately in their next game, away to **Wavertree**. The hosts opted to bat first and, despite an inspired spell of bowling from Sam Williamson (3-30) to remove the top three batsmen, an unbeaten century from Adam Carus McDonald helped Wavertree to a total of 221-5. Rainhill responded positively, with captain Mark Viggars hitting an unbeaten 61, but the visitors finished on162-5 as the teams settled for a draw.

**Phil Morgan**

Despite losing only one of the previous five games, the inability to secure wins meant that Rainhill found themselves just above the relegation zone before the visit of **Highfield**. Highfield won the toss and elected to bat, but soon found themselves in real trouble as Sam Williamson (4-18) and Phil Morgan (4-27) took the opening four wickets for the cost of just two runs. Craig Aspey spearheaded something of a fightback, hitting a resolute unbeaten 53; however, batsmen came and went quickly and only Elliot Gaskell managed to reach double figures as the visitors stumbled to 103 all out. Those present had witnessed an excellent display of pace bowling from Williamson and Morgan.

Rainhill's response also got off to a dreadful start and they slipped to 8-3 before Owen Groom (20) and Joe Harvey (25) made progress against some useful Highfield bowling. Adam Edwards also made an unbeaten contribution of 24 runs as Rainhill reached their target for the loss of seven wickets. It had been a hard-fought win, but a fully merited and very welcome one.

The scheduled home match against strugglers **Spring View** was rained off, meaning Rainhill were denied an opportunity to complete the double over them. The game at **Rainford** began positively for Rainhill and Sam Williamson (3-26), Joe Harvey (3-26) and David Pennington (3-32) had the hosts on the ropes for long periods. Rainford reached a disappointing 121 all out as the visitors once again showed their capabilities in the field, but Rainhill's batting collapsed and they were all out for a dismal 61. Andrew Harrison took a barely believable 6-10 as Rainhill slumped to defeat.

**Adam Edwards**

The Rainford result had once again put Rainhill firmly in relegation trouble with five matches remaining. The match at **Leigh** fell casualty to heavy rain, leaving Rainhill only four games in which to secure their First Division safety. The next challenge was a trip to **Ainsdale** where, in spite of Joe Harvey taking 3-32, the hosts amassed a total of 181-4. It seemed a challenging target for Rainhill, especially when the loss of early wickets had the visitors struggling on 53-5, but a superb partnership between Oliver Powell (56 not out) and David Pennington (61 not out) turned the game on its head and earned an unlikely, but valuable, victory.

**Joe Harvey**

The next match was also away – this time at second placed **Colwyn Bay**. The Welsh side opted to bat first and, despite an outstanding bowling performance from David Pennington (4-45), they were able to reach a total of 188-8 thanks to a spirited knock of 47 from Harry Spillane. Rainhill's reply got off to a difficult start with Jamie Moorhouse (4-41) removing the top four batsmen as the visitors struggled to 52-5. The situation looked desperate for Rainhill but a sixth-wicket partnership between Phil Morgan (42) and David Pennington (32 not out) gave Rainhil hope and began to frustrate the home side. The pair didn't seem in any real trouble until, having taken the score on to 117-5, Morgan played a delivery from Tom Clarke into the hands of Tom O'Melia. The loss of Morgan meant that the run chase was abandoned and saving the game became Rainhill's priority but the loss of Daniel Woodward, Sam Williamson and Sam Addy – all bowled, without scoring, by Clarke – meant that even this seemed unlikely. Stevie Pennington came to the crease with the score at 121-9 and with a little more than 10 overs remaining.

Colwyn Bay's determination to take the final wicket was obvious, but so too was the resilience of Rainhill's tenth wicket pairing. The Penningtons held their resolve and played intelligently to bat out the final ten overs without surrendering the crucial wicket. The duo batted remarkably well under constant pressure and against an experienced bowling attack; they survived a few scares but ultimately emerged unscathed. The game may have ended in a draw but, from Rainhill's perspective, it was a morale-boosting one that definitely felt like a win.

The dramatic draw at Colwyn Bay was followed by a 25-run defeat at home to league leaders **Birkenhead Park**. Rainhill gave a good account of themselves and Joe Harvey took 3-60 as the visitors posted 200-6; in response, Rainhill were all out for 175 although Oliver Powell's 46 and some positive batting from the tail gave the home team reasons to be positive going into their final match against **Northop Hall**.

Prior to the last game of the season Rainhill were one place and 15 points above the relegation zone. Rainhill's fate was in their own hands – if they won, they survived; if not, they needed Wavertree to either beat or draw with Highfield.

Fortunately Rainhill didn't need to concern themselves with results elsewhere. Opting to bat first, Rainhill reached 191-9 with positive contributions from Liam Yate (36), Paul Ford (35), Ethan Powell (31) and Luis Duffy (29). Rainhill then proceeded to bowl

**Stevie Pennington**

Northop Hall out for 132 with David Pennington picking up 3 wickets for 28 runs. A brilliant collective performance had guaranteed league safety and propelled Rainhill to the dizzy heights of seventh place (their highest league position all season).

It had been a frustrating and sometimes difficult season for the 2nd team, with inconsistency being their key problem. However, they were not only able to achieve survival but demonstrated that, on their day, they can compete with the best and achieve results in highly pressurised situations. The match at Colwyn Bay and the games against Old Xaverians and Northop Hall will be remembered for all the right reasons.

**David Pennington**

Similarly, in spite of the fluctuating fortunes of the team, several players had a highly impressive season. Luis Duffy scored over 300 runs including a half-century in the win over Spring View. Phil Morgan continued to show his quality with both bat and ball, while David Pennington emerged as a quality matchwinning all-rounder. 142 runs, including a remarkable unbeaten 61 at Ainsdale, was a good return for a lower-order batsman and he was the leading wicket-taker with 29 victims.

Sam Williamson had an outstanding season, taking 25 wickets at an average of just 15. His quality was obvious and earned him the 2nd team bowling award. No doubt he will continue to progress and, if he continues to perform at this level, will be pushing for a spot in the 1st team in the near future.

The 2nd team can look forward to 2022 with confidence and optimism. They have the makings of a good team and, if they can find some consistency, could well be pushing for promotion.

# LIVERPOOL & DISTRICT CRICKET COMPETITION

## 2ND XI FIRST DIVISION

### Final Standings

| | Pl | w | l | wd | wcn | ld | lcn | d | t | Ab | ND | wc | lc | BatP | BowlP | Pen | Pts |
|---|---|---|---|---|---|---|---|---|---|---|---|---|---|---|---|---|---|
| Colwyn Bay | 22 | 13 | 3 | 0 | 0 | 0 | 0 | 3 | 0 | 2 | 1 | 0 | 0 | 58 | 32 | 0 | 365 |
| Birkenhead Park | 22 | 12 | 3 | 0 | 0 | 0 | 0 | 3 | 0 | 4 | 0 | 0 | 0 | 52 | 38 | 0 | 360 |
| Wigan | 22 | 11 | 5 | 0 | 0 | 0 | 0 | 1 | 0 | 4 | 1 | 0 | 0 | 37 | 24 | 0 | 306 |
| Old Xaverians | 22 | 10 | 3 | 0 | 0 | 0 | 0 | 5 | 0 | 2 | 2 | 0 | 0 | 58 | 21 | 0 | 299 |
| Leigh | 22 | 9 | 5 | 0 | 0 | 0 | 0 | 4 | 0 | 3 | 1 | 0 | 0 | 40 | 52 | 0 | 292 |
| Rainford | 22 | 7 | 9 | 0 | 0 | 0 | 0 | 2 | 0 | 3 | 1 | 0 | 0 | 34 | 40 | 0 | 234 |
| **Rainhill** | **22** | **6** | **7** | **0** | **0** | **0** | **0** | **4** | **0** | **4** | **1** | **0** | **0** | **38** | **40** | **0** | **223** |
| Wavertree | 22 | 5 | 8 | 0 | 0 | 0 | 0 | 3 | 1 | 5 | 0 | 0 | 0 | 42 | 41 | 0 | 223 |
| Northop Hall | 22 | 5 | 9 | 0 | 0 | 0 | 0 | 3 | 0 | 4 | 1 | 0 | 0 | 43 | 46 | 0 | 214 |
| Spring View | 22 | 5 | 10 | 0 | 0 | 0 | 0 | 2 | 0 | 5 | 0 | 0 | 0 | 41 | 42 | 0 | 208 |
| Highfield | 22 | 4 | 13 | 0 | 0 | 0 | 0 | 1 | 1 | 3 | 0 | 0 | 0 | 52 | 36 | 0 | 198 |
| Ainsdale | 22 | 2 | 14 | 0 | 0 | 0 | 0 | 3 | 0 | 3 | 0 | 0 | 0 | 65 | 53 | 0 | 173 |

**Owen Groom and Oliver Powell celebrate a wicket against Wigan**

# SECOND TEAM STATISTICS 2021

## League and Cup matches only

## BATTING

(minimum qualification: 3 innings)

| | Games | Inns | Not Outs | Runs | Top Score | Ave | 50s | 100s | Strike Rate |
|---|---|---|---|---|---|---|---|---|---|
| Luis Duffy | 18 | 17 | 0 | 334 | 53 | 19.7 | 1 | 0 | 70.8 |
| Rob McKeown | 9 | 8 | 2 | 263 | 69* | 43.8 | 3 | 0 | 86.4 |
| Mark Viggars | 13 | 12 | 3 | 237 | 69* | 26.3 | 2 | 0 | 41.2 |
| Phil Morgan | 15 | 12 | 4 | 223 | 50 | 27.9 | 1 | 0 | 60.0 |
| Owen Groom | 16 | 15 | 0 | 212 | 47 | 14.1 | 0 | 0 | 52.9 |
| Liam Yate | 12 | 11 | 0 | 177 | 46 | 16.1 | 0 | 0 | 91.1 |
| Joe Harvey | 13 | 12 | 3 | 155 | 29* | 17.2 | 0 | 0 | 66.5 |
| David Pennington | 17 | 11 | 2 | 142 | 61* | 15.8 | 1 | 0 | 30.0 |
| Adam Edwards | 16 | 13 | 4 | 138 | 31* | 15.3 | 0 | 0 | 95.1 |
| Oliver Powell | 7 | 6 | 1 | 123 | 56* | 24.6 | 1 | 0 | 70.5 |
| Ethan Powell | 8 | 8 | 0 | 88 | 31 | 11.0 | 0 | 0 | 46.1 |
| Jack Ellis | 5 | 5 | 0 | 87 | 68 | 17.4 | 1 | 0 | 47.5 |
| Simon Brown | 7 | 6 | 1 | 77 | 20 | 15.4 | 0 | 0 | 26.9 |
| Sam Williamson | 20 | 14 | 4 | 61 | 18* | 6.1 | 0 | 0 | 39.4 |
| Daniel Woodward | 5 | 4 | 1 | 26 | 14 | 8.7 | 0 | 0 | 37.7 |
| Stevie Pennington | 7 | 6 | 3 | 9 | 4* | 3.0 | 0 | 0 | 18.4 |
| Sam Addy | 5 | 4 | 2 | 0 | 0 | 0.0 | 0 | 0 | 0.0 |

## BOWLING

(minimum qualification: 20 overs)

| | Overs | Maidens | Runs | Wickets | Best Bowling | 5-wicket Haul | Econ Rate | Strike Rate | Ave |
|---|---|---|---|---|---|---|---|---|---|
| David Pennington | 169.2 | 25 | 680 | 29 | 4-36 | 0 | 4.02 | 35.0 | 23.5 |
| Sam Williamson | 127.2 | 29 | 387 | 25 | 4-18 | 0 | 3.04 | 30.6 | 15.5 |
| Phil Morgan | 125.4 | 34 | 368 | 19 | 7-41 | 1 | 2.93 | 39.7 | 19.4 |
| Joe Harvey | 90.0 | 7 | 412 | 15 | 3-26 | 0 | 4.58 | 36.0 | 27.5 |
| Adam Edwards | 63.0 | 11 | 243 | 9 | 2-15 | 0 | 3.86 | 42.0 | 27.0 |
| Jack Ellis | 39.0 | 4 | 139 | 6 | 4-83 | 0 | 4.79 | 29.0 | 23.2 |
| Owen Groom | 56.2 | 10 | 257 | 6 | 2-17 | 0 | 4.56 | 56.3 | 42.8 |
| Luis Duffy | 27.0 | 1 | 125 | 3 | 2-20 | 0 | 4.63 | 54.0 | 41.7 |

**Rainhill 3rd XI v Bootle (h), 29.7.21**

*Back row: Jeff Fitzhenry, Matt Lawler, Adam Lawler, Neil Robinson, Matt Yorke (umpire), Steve Bell, Paul Millar (c), Ethan Powell*
*Front row: Vinny Varghese, Tony Wright, Vishwas Maheshwari, Oliver Powell*

Going into 2021 Rainhill's 3rd team were very much a team in transition. Since the last full season in 2019, some players had moved on or progressed and several new and emerging players were expected to feature regularly. It was difficult to make predictions as to how well the team would do in league competition, but there was a fair amount of optimism that 2021 could be Rainhill's year.

Rainhill kicked off their season away to **Sefton Park PF**—one of two teams Sefton Park Cricket Club had entered into the 3rd XI (Sunday) First Division (South). Sefton Park PF opted to bat first, but lost early wickets as Paul Valentine and Stevie Pennington made life difficult for the top order batsmen. Rainhill felt they were in s strong position when Oliver Bromhead picked up the fourth wicket of the afternoon with only 105 runs on the board, but Sefton Park opener Phil McLoughin (123 not out) and Louis-Jack Prestige (50 not out) turned the game around with an unbeaten partnership of 115.

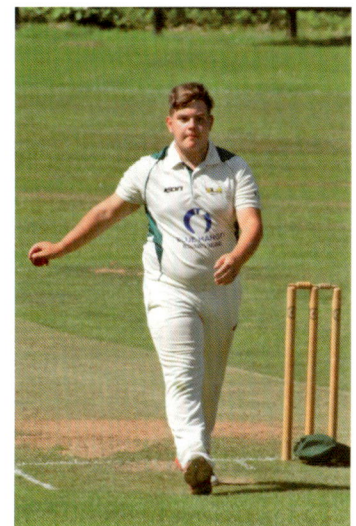

**Paul Valentine**

In pursuit of a target of 221, Rainhill also lost early wickets and were reduced to 4-2 before opener Jeff Fitzhenry (51) and Paul Valentine shared a valuable third-wicket partnership worth 47. After Valentine was out for 25, wicketkeeper Simon Brown joined Fitzhenry and the new pairing took the score on to 118 before Brown was bowled by Ronan Brady, also for 25. The lower order batsmen all contributed something as Rainhill sought to accelerate but the visitors were unable to close in on what was a formidable target and their innings closed with the score on 170-8. Neither team was happy with the draw, but it was probably a fair result.

Rainhill's first home match of the season was against **Merseyside Commonwealth**—a new club playing their first ever game and something of an unknown quantity. Rainhill put Merseyside Commonwealth in to bat and Paul Millar (2-45) made the early breakthrough when he found a way through to Thisara Fernando's pads. After losing the first wicket, Commonwealth wobbled and found themselves on 49-4 before Thushara Withanage (25) and Ichira Yahathugoda (75 not out) inspired their team towards a decent total of 212 all out with some excellent attacking strokeplay. Rainhill bowled well, especially Stevie Pennington (2-35) and Motsim Khan (2-20) but Merseyside Commonwealth had played very positively to recover from the early setbacks.

**Neil Robinson**

Rainhill's run chase was almost successful, spearheaded by Neil Robinson—who scored 93 from 94 balls. Robinson was aided by purposeful knocks from Oliver Bromhead (25), Paul Millar (23) and Stevie Pennington (23) and it looked like Rainhill would pull off a memorable win. Unfortunately for Rainhill, after Robinson was finally out seven runs short of what would have been a fully-deserved century, the team was unable to press on and, despite Rainhill's best efforts, finished just short on 205-8.

Two draws from the opening two games was not an ideal start, but the performance against Merseyside Commonwealth had provided much to be optimistic about. The next match was once again away at Sefton Park—this time to **Sefton Park PS**. Winning the toss and electing to field, Rainhill's Oliver Powell (2-45) dismissed both openers cheaply, but Jack Stirling (53) and Mike Lowe (66) negotiated some disciplined bowling and shared a partnership worth 115 runs. Paul Stirling also played sensibly in his innings of 44 and, despite a flurry of late wickets, Sefton Park PS closed on 232-7. Joe Harvey finished with bowling figures of 3-26—a great performance in the circumstances.

**Ethan Powell**

Rainhill's batsmen struggled to come to terms with the pace bowling of Terry Macklin and Oliver Vasco and soon found themselves in trouble at 19-3. However, Ethan Powell (52) and Joe Harvey (47) provided some entertainment and helped Rainhill back on track, taking the score past 100 before Harvey was trapped lbw by James Orme three runs shy of a half-century. Powell battled on but he ran out of partners as wickets fell at regular intervals. Sefton Park PS dismissed Rainhill for 143 to record a comfortable 89-run victory.

Next up for Rainhill was a home encounter with **Oxton**. Ethan Powell impressed, making 60 from 65 balls, and Tony Wright added a useful 28 but no-one else was able to get into double figures as Rainhill were all out for 123. Defending a low total, Rainhill's bowlers gave Oxton a few scares: a devastating spell of bowling from John Ball (3-5) and the deadly accuracy of Vinny Varghese (2-12) pinned them back and at one point they were on 79-5. Rainhill were unable to maintain the pressure and Oxton eventually secured a three-wicket victory, but they had been made to work hard for it.

Rainhill visited **New Brighton** in the hope of recording their first win of the season. Their innings started dismally as Rainhill's top order collapsed to leave them floundering on 16-4. However, Oliver Powell (41) and Simon Brown (50) led something of a recovery to help Rainhill to a respectable total of 165 all out. New Brighton also got off to a sluggish start as Stevie Pennington dismissed both

**Vinny Varghese**

Stuart Sherratt and Elliot Griffiths for 0 before Iwan Hughes (40) and Oliver Griffiths (57) helped swing the match back in New Brighton's favour. Late wickets for Oliver Powell (2-25) and Charley Partington (1-17) gave Rainhill hope, but New Brighton held their nerve (and rode their luck) to hold on for the win.

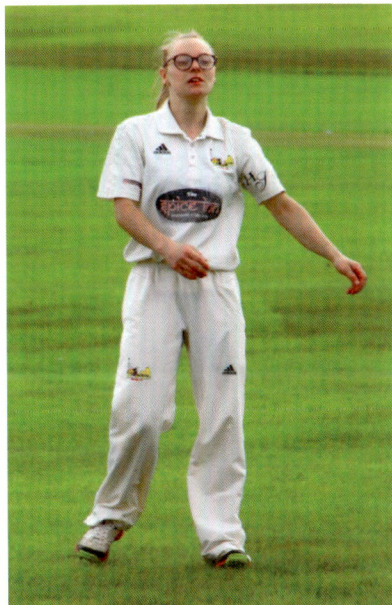
**Charley Partington**

Rainhill's next match was at home to **Sefton Park PF**. Inspired by Oliver Powell who bowled superbly to earn figures of 5-27, Rainhill restricted their opponents to 138 all out. Sam Addy was also effective and economical to take 3-9, with quality fielding backing up the bowlers' efforts. With rain forecast, Rainhill's batsmen scored quickly and accelerated to 80-4, thanks to the efforts of Liam Yate (34) and Panchu Xavier (16 not out). Unfortunately, with the target in sight and with six wickets in hand, the rain arrived. An absolute deluge meant further play was an unrealistic prospect and the match ended in a draw.

The outcome was tough on Rainhill who had set themselves up perfectly and seemed to be cruising towards their first victory of 2021. Victory would also elude them in their next match: a friendly against **Rainhill's Sunday XI**. Both sides' innings finished on 234, but the intra-club friendly did at least provide the opportunity for Panchu Xavier and Neil Robinson to hit unbeaten fifties.

Given their travails in the league, Rainhill welcomed the opportunity for a cup run. In the first round of the Mike Leddy Cup (an LDCC T20 competition) Rainhill were drawn away to **Orrell Red Triangle**. Rainhill did well in the field and in the face of some disciplined bowling (and a couple of spectacular run-outs) Orrell were only able to reach a total of 89-7 from their allotted 20 overs. Paul Millar finished with figures of 2-10 from his 4 overs—an excellent achievement. It wasn't plain sailing for Rainhill's batsmen but Tony Wright (17) and Panchu Xavier (29) got the team off to a good start in pursuit of the target, which was reached with more than 3 overs to spare.

Having earned a valuable win in cup action, Rainhill followed it up with an even better one in the league away at **Whitefield**. The hosts opted to bat first but within minutes the two openers were back in the pavilion, having both been bowled by Stevie Pennington without scoring. A devastating spell of bowling from Pennington, who took 4-6, had Whitefield on the ropes. Matthew Connolly (20) and Kevin Connolly (26) played sensibly and their efforts helped Whitefield move towards the hundred mark, but Rainhill's bowlers continued to apply pressure and wickets fell regularly. Steve Bell took 2-17 while John Ball (0-2 from 5 overs), Sarah Curlett (1-12) and Oliver Powell (1-16) bowled tightly to deny scoring opportunities. Whitefield were eventually all out for 121.

**John Ball bowling during the match at Whitefield**

Whitefield's opening bowlers Ben Ashcroft (2-27) and Ben Thomas (2-38) gave their team belief as Tony Wright (8), Stevie Pennington (5) and Kiran Nair (0) all struggled to come to terms with their line and pace. With Rainhill on 14-3 Ethan Powell (18) and Oliver Powell (40) came together and they added 50 for the fourth wicket, a collective effort that helped turn the match firmly in Rainhill's favour. Oliver Powell was then joined by Paul Valentine, whose unbeaten 35 from 28 deliveries included three sixes and made victory inevitable.

Rainhill faced Whitefield again in their next league game, but sandwiched between those two matches was the Mike Leddy Cup match at home to **Bootle**. Steve Bell (2-27) and Neil Robinson (2-18) took two wickets each, while Tony Wright showed his value with an excellent stumping to dismiss Joash Vinu. Bootle finished their innings on 149-6 but Rainhill will have felt reasonably happy with their efforts in the field.

Rainhill's top order struggled to score at the required rate and wickets fell rapidly. Rainhill were on 55-5 before Ethan Powell (39) and Oliver Powell (37 not out) came together; the brothers played valiantly to restore some pride even if the required run rate proved beyond them. They helped Rainhill reach 119-6 from their 20 overs and showed maturity and creativity in the way they approached the game.

Following their cup exit, Rainhill hosted **Whitefield,** against whom they had recorded their first league win two weekends previously. Whitefield proved much tougher opposition on this occasion with Matthew Connolly (53) and Rob Kennerly (24) guiding the visitors to 159 all out. John Ball (3-17) and Paul Millar (2-35) continually created problems for Whitefield, while Sarah Curlett (2-27) demonstrated her potential as a useful

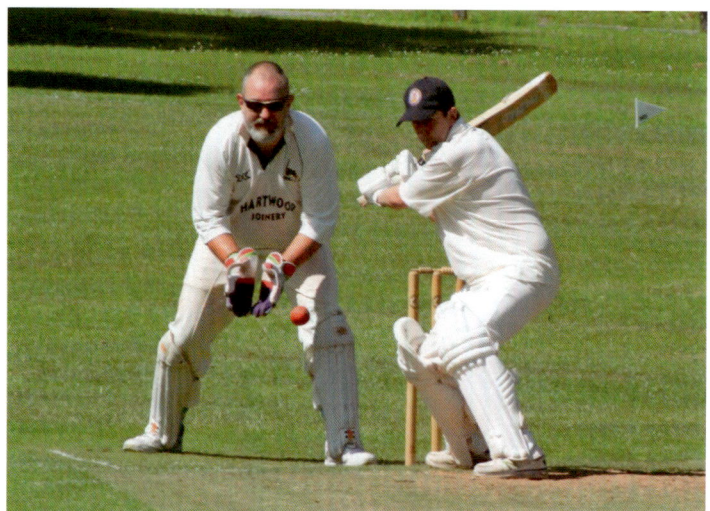

**Wicketkeeper Tony Wright**

attacking bowler. It was a good all-round team performance in the field against a side much improved from the previous encounter. Chasing 160, solid contributions from Jeff Fitzhenry (28) and Ethan Powell (18) helped to build a platform before Panchu Xavier (35) and Paul Millar (37 not out) raced towards the target. Their fluent strokeplay was a joy to watch and Millar looked at ease finding gaps in the field, much to Whitefield's frustration. Rainhill's third win in four matches lifted them to sixth place in the league and out of the relegation zone.

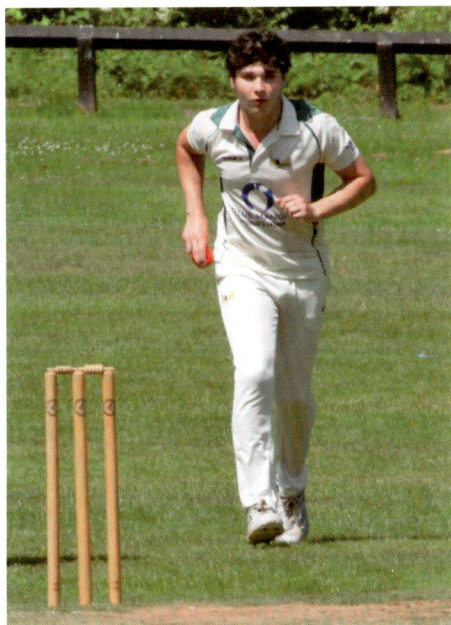

**Paul Millar**

The home match to second-placed **Sefton Park PS** was abandoned due to heavy rain. The next match, away to league leaders **Oxton**, was a bad-tempered affair that Rainhill came within a whisker of winning. Neil Robinson (60) and Simon Brown (54 not out) helped Rainhill to a creditable 207-8 before Oxton—after a decent start—found themselves in disarray after a stunning spell from Stevie Pennington (4-31) swept away their middle order. With Oxton on 158-7, Rainhill sensed their opportunity but were unable to dislodge Mike Baker (54 not out) and the resilient Gunasekeran Kumar (25 not out). It was a frustrating and disappointing conclusion, but the strong performance against the leaders underlined the team's growing confidence.

**Bootle** were the next visitors to Victoria Terrace. They put Rainhill in to bat and the home team reached 148 all out. Jeff Fitzhenry, Ethan Powell and Matt Lawler all scored 28 as several players made positive starts but failed to build on them. This was also true for Bootle, who never looked entirely comfortable against Rainhill's attack. John Ball was particularly impressive, taking 5-39, and he was ably supported by Oliver Powell and Stevie Pennington who bowled economically and restricted the flow of runs. When Tony Wright stumped Cyril Paul for 33 off the bowling of Vinny Varghese, Bootle were on 112-7 and the game was on a knife-edge. Rainhill took another wicket but Bootle's Paul Jones (35 not out) and Matthew Medlicott held out and for the win.

**Oliver Powell**

In two successive matches Rainhill had come so close to victory but had been unable to seize the opportunity. With three games left in the season the team was determined to finish on a high. Unfortunately, only one of these games went ahead as New Brighton and Bootle conceded their matches because of issues with ground availability. This ensured Rainhill finished in the top half of the table and also meant their final match of 2021 would be at **Merseyside Commonwealth**.

The hosts batted first, with Sam Wayne (44) and Suraj Bandara (38) making headway against some determined Rainhill bowling before Oliver Powell (3-20) triggered a middle order collapse as six wickets fell for just 34 runs. In trouble on 139-9, a spirited tenth-wicket partnership between Ichira Yahathugoda (47 not out) and Jehan Yahathugoda (29) added 67 runs before Neil Robinson struck to remove the latter's leg stump. Merseyside Commonweath were all out for 206 — but how crucial would that last-wicket partnership prove?

Rainhill lost three early wickets but purposeful and determine knocks from Panchu Xavier (80 from 77 balls) and Paul Millar (51 from 74) put Rainhill in a strong position. The duo shared a 97-run fifth-wicket partnership and, after Millar was expertly stumped just after reaching his half-century, Xavier and Vinny Varghese (31 not out from 35 balls) sought to pull off a dramatic victory. Agonisingly for Rainhill, the audacious charge towards the ambitious target fell just short. Rainhill ended their innings on 204-7 and had to be content with a draw.

The match summed up the 3rd team's season: courageous efforts combined with missed opportunities leading to frustrating results. However, the team can be proud of a third-placed finish after a stuttering start to the league campaign and that will be something to build on in the coming season. With talented young players like Stevie Pennington, Sam Addy, Sarah Curlett, Lucy Strettle and the Powell brothers the future looks bright, while Steve Bell, Paul Millar, Jeff Fitzhenry, John Ball and Panchu Xavier bring maturity and no shortage of skill. Under the captaincy of Matt Lawler, will the magic formula of youth and experience spell success for Rainhill in 2022?

**Amber Bowie and Lucy Strettle**

**LIVERPOOL & DISTRICT CRICKET COMPETITION**

**3RD XI (SUNDAY) FIRST DIVISION (SOUTH)**

**Final Standings**

| | Pl | w | l | wd | wcn | ld | lcn | d | t | Ab | ND | wc | lc | BatP | BowlP | Pen | Pts |
|---|---|---|---|---|---|---|---|---|---|---|---|---|---|---|---|---|---|
| Oxton | 14 | 10 | 2 | 0 | 1 | 0 | 0 | 1 | 0 | 0 | 0 | 0 | 0 | 14 | 35 | 0 | 274 |
| Sefton Park (PS) | 14 | 8 | 2 | 0 | 0 | 0 | 0 | 1 | 0 | 3 | 0 | 0 | 0 | 28 | 26 | 0 | 229 |
| **Rainhill** | **14** | **2** | **5** | **0** | **2** | **0** | **0** | **3** | **0** | **1** | **1** | **0** | **0** | **31** | **38** | **0** | **169** |
| Bootle | 14 | 3 | 4 | 0 | 1 | 0 | 1 | 2 | 0 | 2 | 1 | 0 | 0 | 23 | 14 | 0 | 127 |
| Merseyside C'th | 14 | 2 | 2 | 0 | 1 | 0 | 2 | 4 | 0 | 3 | 0 | 0 | 0 | 33 | 17 | 5 | 105 |
| New Brighton | 14 | 2 | 2 | 0 | 1 | 0 | 2 | 5 | 0 | 1 | 1 | 0 | 0 | 37 | 18 | 5 | 105 |
| Sefton Park (PF) | 14 | 1 | 6 | 0 | 0 | 0 | 0 | 4 | 0 | 2 | 1 | 0 | 0 | 32 | 36 | 0 | 103 |
| Whitefield | 14 | 2 | 7 | 0 | 0 | 0 | 1 | 2 | 0 | 2 | 0 | 0 | 0 | 26 | 21 | 0 | 87 |

**Steve Bell (left) and Sam Addy (right)**

# THIRD TEAM STATISTICS 2021

## League and Cup matches only

## BATTING

(minimum qualification: 3 innings)

| | Games | Inns | Not Outs | Runs | Top Score | Ave | 50s | 100s | Strike Rate |
|---|---|---|---|---|---|---|---|---|---|
| Ethan Powell | 11 | 11 | 0 | 248 | 60 | 22.6 | 2 | 0 | 64.3 |
| Neil Robinson | 8 | 8 | 1 | 214 | 93 | 30.6 | 2 | 0 | 84.2 |
| Panchu Xavier | 5 | 5 | 1 | 166 | 80 | 41.5 | 1 | 0 | 97.2 |
| Jeff Fitzhenry | 12 | 10 | 1 | 154 | 51 | 17.1 | 1 | 0 | 37.9 |
| Paul Millar | 8 | 7 | 1 | 130 | 51 | 21.7 | 1 | 0 | 74.3 |
| Simon Brown | 3 | 3 | 1 | 129 | 54* | 64.5 | 2 | 0 | 69.3 |
| Oliver Powell | 8 | 7 | 1 | 124 | 41 | 20.7 | 0 | 0 | 61.7 |
| Vinny Varghese | 7 | 7 | 2 | 86 | 31 | 17.2 | 0 | 0 | 66.3 |
| Tony Wright | 6 | 6 | 0 | 74 | 28 | 12.3 | 0 | 0 | 90.3 |
| Stevie Pennington | 12 | 9 | 2 | 71 | 23 | 10.1 | 0 | 0 | 32.4 |
| John Ball | 6 | 4 | 2 | 61 | 32* | 30.5 | 0 | 0 | 70.1 |
| Matt Lawler | 4 | 3 | 0 | 31 | 28 | 10.3 | 0 | 0 | 51.7 |
| Sam Addy | 6 | 4 | 0 | 17 | 9 | 4.3 | 0 | 0 | 29.0 |
| Sarah Curlett | 6 | 3 | 1 | 13 | 13 | 6.5 | 0 | 0 | 48.2 |
| Lucy Strettle | 3 | 3 | 0 | 7 | 6 | 2.3 | 0 | 0 | 8.3 |
| Adam Lawler | 5 | 3 | 2 | 4 | 3* | 4.0 | 0 | 0 | 14.8 |

## BOWLING

(minimum qualification: 20 overs)

| | Overs | Maidens | Runs | Wickets | Best Bowling | 5-wicket Haul | Econ Rate | Strike Rate | Ave |
|---|---|---|---|---|---|---|---|---|---|
| Oliver Powell | 45.0 | 8 | 185 | 14 | 5-27 | 1 | 4.11 | 19.3 | 13.2 |
| Stevie Pennington | 77.5 | 10 | 281 | 14 | 4-6 | 0 | 3.61 | 33.4 | 20.1 |
| John Ball | 52.4 | 15 | 136 | 12 | 5-39 | 1 | 2.58 | 26.3 | 11.3 |
| Paul Millar | 53.0 | 3 | 222 | 11 | 2-10 | 0 | 4.19 | 28.9 | 20.2 |
| Steve Bell | 32.0 | 1 | 160 | 9 | 3-71 | 0 | 5.00 | 21.3 | 17.8 |
| Vinny Varghese | 37.3 | 1 | 143 | 8 | 2-12 | 0 | 3.81 | 28.1 | 17.9 |
| Sam Addy | 34.5 | 1 | 190 | 6 | 3-9 | 0 | 5.45 | 34.8 | 31.7 |
| Sarah Curlett | 27.0 | 1 | 133 | 3 | 2-27 | 0 | 4.93 | 54.0 | 44.3 |

# THE SUNDAY TEAM'S TALE

**Rainhill Sunday XI v Bury (h), 25.7.21**

*Back row: Joe Crossley (c), Richard Appleton, Matt Yorke (umpire), Paul Millar, Neil Robinson, Kiran Nair, Vinny Varghese, Oliver Powell, David Crossley (scorer).*
*Front row: Matt Lawler, Tony Wright, Sam Addy, Stuart Brown*

In addition to the three senior competitive teams, Rainhill Cricket Club has for many years run a "Sunday team", playing only friendly matches and focused on recreational cricket. Its main purposes are twofold: to aid the development of young players and to provide an opportunity for everyone to play irrespective of ability.

The Sunday XI is perfect for those of us who are learning to play cricket, who have physical limitations, who prefer the more leisurely approach or who simply dislike the cut and thrust that is a common feature of fierce competition. Sunday cricket is nothing if not inclusive. Sunday matches are where fathers play with sons (and sometimes daughters), where the umpire is the batsman who was last out and, crucially, where everyone gets a chance to play however unselectable they may appear. It's also where you're surprised by the consistent line and length of the sexagenarian bowler, impressed by the fielding of young teenagers or awed by the strokeplay of ageing campaigners. It's unrehearsed theatre, even if the cast is far from stellar. Sunday cricket is where players are born, and where they ultimately return.

Like all sports teams, Sunday cricket sides are a sum of their individual parts. However, such a statement diminishes the role one key person plays: the captain. Sunday captains don't merely motivate players and take a leadership role on the field. They mentor young players. They coax older ones ("just another season, Jack!"). They organise fixtures and transport. They spend their week frantically telephoning everyone in the hope that, by some miracle, they can find 11 people for the next game. And then they have the near impossible task of keeping everyone happy, while trying to forge a team from an array of players with different levels and abilities – all of whom could realistically be taken by the seconds or thirds next week, especially if they play too well.

Rainhill's Sunday XI captain is Joe Crossley. His age is the nearest thing to a state secret, but he's been a player at the club since the late 1970s, and had been playing in Staffordshire for several years before that. Joe is the personification of Sunday cricket – straightforward but unpredictable, quirky yet endearing, fair-minded but enigmatic. In addition to being the nearest thing to a national expert there is on the history of the Staffordshire Club Cricket Championship, Joe is a passionate champion of Sunday cricket, to which he has given the last 40 years or so of his life.

In 2021 he once again offered his services as Sunday team captain. Why does he do it? Because he absolutely believes in it: in its values, its ethos and its undeniable place at the centre of the amateur game. And, if he's being honest, he'd tell you it's because he absolutely loves it.

**Joe Crossley**

Success for the Sunday team is probably not best measured in the same way as it is for competitive sides. It would be wrong to suggest that winning is not a motivation, but it is secondary to providing opportunity. The Sunday team was fielding female players long before Rainhill had a women's team. There are several players in its ranks who it is perhaps diplomatic to describe as veterans. It contains players with disabilities. It fields youngsters who want to make the step-up into senior cricket but perhaps aren't yet ready for the 3rd team. Basically, it gives games to people who may otherwise not be able to enjoy playing cricket.

In the club's 150th anniversary season it seems fitting to celebrate the Sunday team's ongoing commitment to facilitating recreational cricket at a time when many other clubs have long since axed their friendly teams. Rainhill Cricket Club is committed to advancing inclusivity and diversity, and the Sunday team is one way in which it achieves this.

**The Sunday team at Prescot**

The Sunday XI began their season with a 5-wicket victory at **Hightown St-Mary's**, thanks to a magnificent knock of 57 from Stevie Pennington, a regular player for the under-15s playing in his first senior match. They then entertained **Old Parkonians** and, despite strong bowling performances from John Doyle (3-51) and Scott Clegg (1-30), Rainhill struggled to get anywhere near the target of 177 and were all out for 96. Several players contributed runs but none were able to stay at the crease for long enough to build an innings.

The Sunday team visited **Colwyn Bay** in May. It was a highlight of the season for many Sunday team players to perform at Penrhyn Avenue, a fantastic venue that has often been used for County Championship matches (as recently as 2019, for Glamorgan v Lancashire). It was an even better feeling to come away with a result against Colwyn Bay's 3rd team—who had not, until this point, lost a match all season. Colwyn Bay's Nick Bould (29) and Matt Russell (64 not out) got the Welshmen off to a fine start and scored quickly, but they were pegged back by some excellent bowling and unusually brilliant fielding. From 102-1, Colwyn Bay slumped to 164-8, and were eventually all out for 191. Neil Robinson took 5-27 from just 4.3 overs.

The target seemed a tall order but a half-century from Tony Wright and an outstanding unbeaten 48 from Steve Bell helped Joe Crossley's friendly team defeat a very strong Colwyn Bay 3rd string side by 5 wickets. It was a terrific result and one that will not be forgotten quickly.

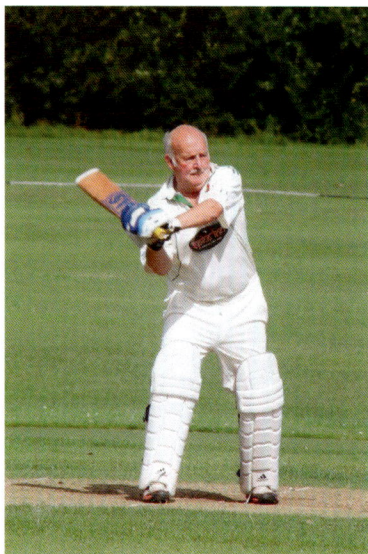

**Richard Appleton**

In June Rainhill played host to **Prescot & Odyssey**, a clash of two teams in which historical local rivalry is always in the background irrespective of the level of competition. Spinners Vishwas Maheshwari (3-14) and Scott Clegg (1-13) impressed, as did medium pacer Paul Millar (3-15), and Prescot were bowled out for 135. Stand-in wicketkeeper Richard Appleton did a sterling job behind the stumps and Kristopher Duffin took a terrific catch to end the innings. Samuel Waine batted effectively and patiently for the visitors in his innings of 40, but at the interval Rainhill felt they had the upper hand.

However, it was a similar story for Rainhill with Neil Robinson playing intelligently to reach 38 and other players chipping in but finding it difficult to stay at the crease for long. Prescot used six bowlers, all of whom took wickets, as the Sunday team were all out for 123. It had been a close match and Rainhill were disappointed not to have been able to make it two wins on the bounce.

The Sunday team did win their next two games, however. The first of these, the annual match at **Frodsham**, was won by the margin of 128 runs. Replying to Rainhill's 190 all out, Frodsham only made 62 as Steve Bell (5-11) and John Doyle (2-11) produced some scintillating bowling. The next game was a T20 match against **Old Parkonians**, who had already comfortably beaten the Sunday team earlier in the season. Old Parkonians batted first and notched up 137-2 from their 20 overs, a reasonably impressive performance; however, Rainhill were able to chase down the target with seven balls to spare. Matt Lawler (48) and Vinny Varghese (66) frustrated a strong Old Parkonians attack and steered their team to a superb and thoroughly deserved victory.

The Sunday XI played out a tied match with Rainhill's 3rd team before welcoming **Liverpool Superkings** to Victoria Terrace for a midweek T20, a match Rainhill won by 8 wickets. This was followed by a four-wicket home defeat by **Bury** that was highly competitive and played in an excellent spirit. Oliver Powell top scored with 40 as the Sunday team amassed 175 from 40 overs, but it wasn't quite enough as Bury recovered from 95-5 to chase down the target with just over three overs left to play. Sam Addy bowled well for Rainhill, taking 2-50 and demonstrating his quality as a spinner.

**Stuart Brown**

In the home match against Formby, Joe Crossley brought Sam Ellis, Amber Bowie and Thomas Lewis into the side. Batting first, Richard Appleton, Asif Junaid, Adam Lawler and Stuart Brown all made positive starts but found it difficult to live with the relentless accuracy of Formby's bowling, especially Nicholas Androulidakis (3-6). Rainhill struggled to 110-9, but the visitors also found the going tough. Adam Lawler (2-22), Asif Junaid (1-11) and Stuart Brown (1-17) ensured a gripping contest between bat and ball. Kristopher Duffin also took his first wicket for the Sunday team, but Formby were able to press on to reach their target with four wickets in hand.

Rainhill got back to winning ways against **Prestwich** in another close encounter at Victoria Terrace. Paul Millar starred with the ball, finishing with 4-9, but it was an all-round team performance in the field that helped the hosts bowl out Prestwich for 105. In a low-scoring game contributions of 26 from Oliver Powell and Neil Robinson proved valuable and ultimately match-winning. Prestwich caused all kinds of trouble for Rainhill's batters and the home side were relieved when Steve Bell hit the runs to secure a narrow two-wicket victory. Who says Sunday cricket isn't competitive?

**Ned Brougham**

The Sunday team's final match of the season was at home to the same team they had played on the opening day: **Hightown St Mary's**. It was a very different Rainhill team that was fielded on this occasion, with Motsim Khan drafted in as wicketkeeper and juniors Kieran Rose and Ollie Unsworth making appearances. Rainhill won the toss and elected to bat, but unfortunately collapsed from 25-0 to 29-4 and never fully recovered. They rallied a little bit thanks to a useful partnership between Deepak Gupta and Kristopher Duffin, but once they were out Rainhill offered little resistance and were bowled out for 74.

Rainhill's bowling attack was spearheaded by Ned Brougham (0-14) and Lucy Strettle (2-13), who bowled to put pressure on Hightown St Mary's from the start. Scott Clegg (3-13) and Deepak Gupta (1-5 from 7 overs) not only took wickets but slowed the run rate down to a trickle. Hightown St Mary's had time on their side but, with wickets falling rapidly and the score on 54-6, knew they had to push on. Turab Ali (15 not out) and Akshay Bhatnagar rose to the challenge and saw their team over the line, but it had been yet another very evenly-matched contest.

At the end of an eventful season for the Sunday team a decision was taken to create a new 4th team to play in a Sunday league and for the Sunday team to rebrand as "Rainhill Recreationals". Joe Crossley will continue to captain the recreational team, which will remain focused on providing opportunities for everyone who wants to play cricket. The Recreationals will play only friendly games but it is anticipated that they will have more matches in 2022 and will play a broader range of similarly-minded teams from across the North West.

# THE WOMEN'S TALE

**Rainhill Women Super 8s v Wavertree (h), 9.6.21**

*Back row: Sue Lowrie, Sarah Curlett, Katie Roberts, Chloe Gillespie, Susan Rotheram*
*Front row: Julie Foulkes, Vicky Graham, Rachel Court*

Rainhill's women played in both hardball and softball competitions in three different leagues during 2021. In what was their first full season (2020 being severely reduced due to the pandemic) Rainhill made significant progress, especially in softball cricket.

They also entered the Lancashire T20 competition and, while they were comprehensively beaten by Sefton Park and Hightown St Mary's, they will have learned from the experience of playing two of the best sides in the area.

Rather than take a chronological overview of the season, a difficult task given the lack of statistical data on Play Cricket, it's probably easiest to take a more general look at how the women's team fared in each of their league competitions.

They began life in the LDCC Super 8s Hardball League with a close-run contest at home to Wavertree. The visitors posted 288-2 (a net score of 478); in reply Rainhill finished with a creditable 282-8 (net score 242). It was a promising showing, most notable for Sue Lowrie's performance as

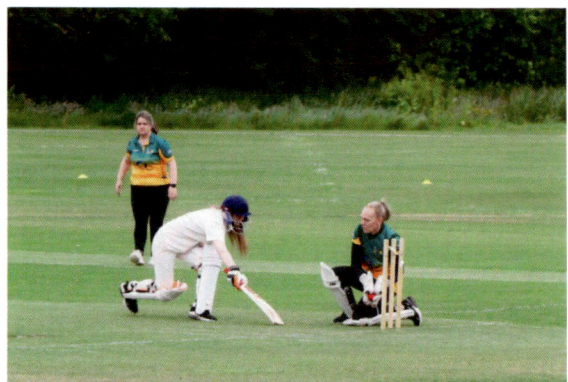

**Sue Lowrie attempts a run-out versus Wavertree**

wicketkeeper and some powerful batting from Chloe Gillespie and Sarah Curlett. The close match against Wavertree was followed by a battle against Liverpool that was anything but, although once again Rainhill could take positives from they way they played: Katie Roberts hit 22 from 16 balls and Amber Bowie took 2-11.

**Sarah Curlett**

Rainhill then came up against Tarleton and it was another very close encounter between two evenly-matched teams. Lucy Brown (26) and Sarah Curlett (32) showed their batting potential and helped Rainhill to a total of 100-5 (net score 275). Amber Bowie (1-12), Lucy Brown (1-15) and Katie Roberts (1-17) all took a wicket as Tarleton could only make 87-3 (net score 272). There were just three runs in it!

The win gave Rainhill a much needed boost ahead of their match with Bootle. Katie Roberts and Lily Murphy picked up a wicket apiece but Bootle raced to 116-2 (net score 306). Sarah Curlett (11) and Susan Rotheram (9) led the reply but Rainhill were not able to keep up with the required run rate and could only reach 77-3 from their allotted 16 overs. However, the batting looked solid and Bootle had to work hard for their wickets.

Rainhill conceded their match against Sefton Park meaning their next match was against Hightown St Mary's. Rainhill eased to 77-1 (net score 272) before reducing Hightown to 95-5 (net score 234). It was the best hardball performance of the year and Rainhill surprised themselves with the nature of the win and the margin of victory.

Rainhill finished their hardball campaign with two wins from their six games—an excellent effort given the fact it was their first season in the league. The team had showed themselves capable of playing some excellent cricket and beating well-drilled sides. A fifth placed finish was a

**Bobbie Grant**

satisfactory return for their efforts and the team will hope to build on that in 2022.

Rainhill fared even better in softball. After some tricky opening games in the LDCC Super 8s Softball League, Rainhill recorded an excellent win against Hightown St Mary's and followed this up with a narrow victory over Fleetwood Hesketh. Batting first, Rainhill's Bobbie Grant (10), Susan Rotheram (11), Sue Lowrie (15) and Carol Bates (14) all made solid contributions as they reached a total of 90-2 (net score 280). Fleetwood Hesketh had little difficulty in staying just ahead of the required run rate, but they were pinned back as Rainhill took key wickets. Katie Roberts (1-12) and Jess Bates (2-12) were the pick of the bowlers and looked dangerous while giving very little away. In the final analysis, the additional wickets proved vital: Fleetwood closed their innings on 92—one run more than Rainhill but, once wickets were deducted, with a net score of 271.

Aside from the matches they won, Rainhill had some other excellent games where they fell just short. In their meeting with Skelmersdale, Vicky Graham proved the star with both bat and ball, taking 2-7 in a game that looked to be going Rainhill's way until Skelmersdale captain Kirstie Hunter hit 27 in 15 deliveries at the end. There was also a close-run match at Moor Park, where Julie Foulkes (2-11) and Katie

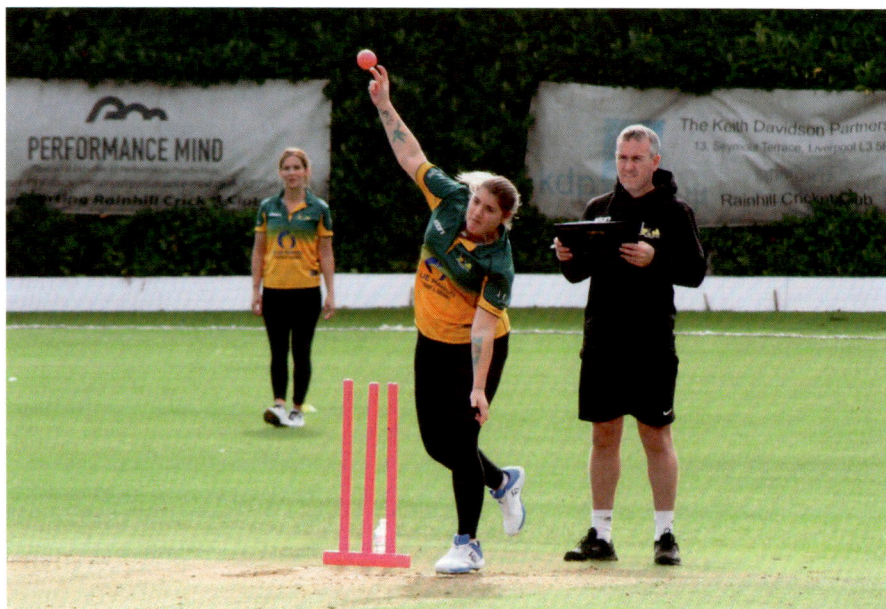

**Vicky Graham**

Roberts (2-17) put in a brilliant performance as Rainhill took on Northern. Northern closed their innings after posting 104-5 (net score 279) and Rainhill got off to a good start thanks to the batting of Lucy Strettle and Amber Bowie. Unfortunately Rainhill lost their momentum towards the end of their innings as Gabby Westbury and Nicola Reeves took four wickets between them, and their chase petered out. Rainhill ended on 87-7 (net score 252) but once again they had shown that they could compete against strong opposition.

As in the Super 8s Hardball League, Rainhill left their best performance until the final day of the competition. At home to Bootle Belles B, Rainhill were looking for a win that would lift them out of the bottom two. Rainhill started well, taking three wickets in the first three overs, before Bootle fought their way back into the game to reach 82-3 (net score 267). Rainhill's pursuit began with Vicky Graham and Katie Roberts leading the charge, hitting 21 without loss in the first four overs. Liv Reilly and Chloe Gillespie then continued to keep the runs flowing. The next pairing, Susan Rotheram and Bobbie Grant, found it more difficult to score as Bootle adjusted the field and began to exert pressure. However, the Rainhill pair responded well, typified by a classy cover drive from Susan Rotheram.

Lucy Strettle and Julie Foulkes were the last to bat for Rainhill. Closing in on the target, Rainhill looked favourites to win until Strettle was caught at short fine leg, taking five runs from the total. A fraught final couple of overs ensued, with Rainhill looking to get bat on ball and Bootle bowling some fantasic deliveries, much to the home side's frustration. It was nervous but Strettle and Foulkes denied Bootle a further crucial wicket and scored the runs to secure a well-earned victory. The joy of their watching teammates was tangible - and, indeed, audible.

Lucy Brown said that the game showed "our batting has improved so much" while Bobbie Grant felt that the match was "the best we've played as a team".

Vicky Graham said: "It was a close match. We did well opening out with 21 and we've progressed a lot since the start of the season. We're much more tactically aware now and we've learned how to adjust our batting against certain bowlers. I think other teams have seen us as an easy win, but we proved ourselves today.

"Bootle are a good team and for us to beat them is fantastic. We needed this - it's a great ending for 2021 and gives us a massive boost for next season. We have shown we are competitive and will give it our all. "

Indeed they did, and the teams was pleased with a ninth placed finish (out of 13 teams). With the experience of a full league campaign behind them, they will aspire to do even better in 2022.

Rainhill's women were most successful, however, in the LDCC Softball League. Amazingly, Rainhill won eight of their opening nine matches, recording excellent victories over Rainford (twice), Newton-le-Willows, Mawdesley, Maghull, Liverpool, Sefton Park and Northern. The only match they lost from those opening nine was the reverse fixture against Mawdesley and they looked like serious title contenders. Indeed, Rainhill were one of only two teams to beat Mawdesley all season. Unfortunately for Rainhill, they lost their final three games of the season, including a one-run defeat to Sefton Park, and had to be content with second place.

Despite the end to the league campaign, finishing runner-up to champions Mawdesley represented a significant achievement in its own right. For a team that didn't exist two years ago—consisting of several players who hadn't even picked up a bat before then—it was a marker of how far they have come in a short time.

At the end of season awards, Julie Foulkes won the most improved player award. The batting award went to Bobbie Grant while Susan Rotheram took the bowling award. Sue Lowrie won the players' player of a year award and was clearly a popular choice.

2021 was a season of significant progress for Rainhill's women. On the field they won some key matches, have developed as a team and have made significant progress especially in softball cricket. They are undoubtedly an emerging force. Off the field they have been credited with helping the club become more inclusive and diverse. Club President Peter Mercer said: "Thinking about the year more generally one of the massive successes was the smooth integration of the girls and women's teams into the club. For me it changed the feel and atmosphere of the club in a very positive way."

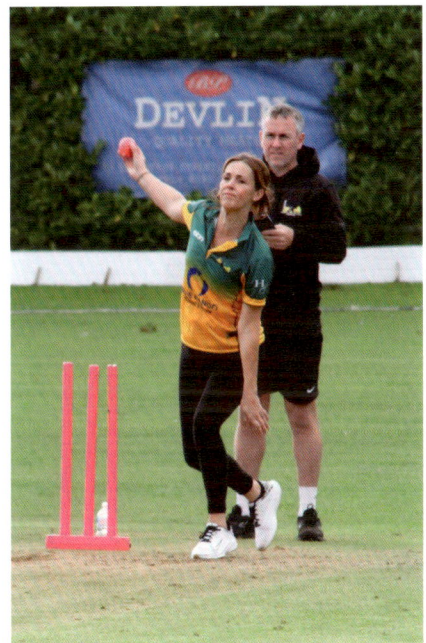

**Susan Rotheram**

**LIVERPOOL & DISTRICT CRICKET COMPETITION**

**SUPER 8s HARDBALL LEAGUE**

**Final Standings**

| | Pl | w | l | c | a | t | wcn | lcn | Pen | Pts |
|---|---|---|---|---|---|---|---|---|---|---|
| Sefton Park | 6 | 5 | 0 | 0 | 0 | 0 | 1 | 0 | 0 | 18 |
| Bootle | 6 | 5 | 1 | 0 | 0 | 0 | 0 | 0 | 0 | 15 |
| Hightown | 6 | 1 | 3 | 0 | 0 | 0 | 2 | 0 | 0 | 9 |
| Liverpool | 6 | 2 | 3 | 0 | 0 | 0 | 1 | 0 | 0 | 9 |
| **Rainhill** | **6** | **2** | **3** | **0** | **0** | **0** | **0** | **1** | **0** | **5** |
| Wavertree | 6 | 1 | 3 | 1 | 0 | 0 | 0 | 1 | 0 | 3 |
| Tarleton | 6 | 0 | 3 | 1 | 0 | 0 | 0 | 2 | 0 | 1 |

# LIVERPOOL & DISTRICT CRICKET COMPETITION
## SUPER 8s SOFTBALL LEAGUE
### Final Standings

| | Pl | w | l | c | a | t | wcn | lcn | Pen | Pts |
|---|---|---|---|---|---|---|---|---|---|---|
| Sefton Park | 12 | 10 | 0 | 0 | 1 | 0 | 1 | 0 | 0 | 34 |
| Southport & Birkdale | 12 | 10 | 2 | 0 | 0 | 0 | 0 | 0 | 0 | 30 |
| Liverpool | 12 | 9 | 3 | 0 | 0 | 0 | 0 | 0 | 0 | 27 |
| Northern | 12 | 9 | 3 | 0 | 0 | 0 | 0 | 0 | 0 | 27 |
| Bootle A | 12 | 7 | 3 | 0 | 1 | 0 | 1 | 0 | 0 | 25 |
| Skelmersdale | 12 | 6 | 6 | 0 | 0 | 0 | 0 | 0 | 0 | 18 |
| Maghull | 12 | 6 | 5 | 0 | 0 | 0 | 0 | 1 | 0 | 17 |
| Old Xaverians | 12 | 4 | 6 | 0 | 1 | 0 | 1 | 0 | 0 | 16 |
| **Rainhill** | **12** | **3** | **8** | **1** | **0** | **0** | **0** | **0** | **0** | **10** |
| Bootle B | 12 | 3 | 9 | 0 | 0 | 0 | 0 | 0 | 0 | 9 |
| Tarleton | 12 | 3 | 7 | 1 | 0 | 0 | 0 | 1 | 0 | 9 |
| Hightown St Mary's | 12 | 2 | 9 | 0 | 1 | 0 | 0 | 0 | 0 | 7 |
| Fleetwood Hesketh | 12 | 0 | 11 | 0 | 0 | 0 | 0 | 1 | 0 | 1 |

# LIVERPOOL & DISTRICT CRICKET COMPETITION
## WOMEN'S SOFTBALL LEAGUE
### Final Standings

| | Pl | w | l | c | a | t | wcn | lcn | Pen | Pts |
|---|---|---|---|---|---|---|---|---|---|---|
| Mawdesley | 12 | 9 | 2 | 0 | 0 | 0 | 1 | 0 | 0 | 30 |
| **Rainhill** | **12** | **8** | **4** | **0** | **0** | **0** | **0** | **0** | **0** | **24** |
| Northern | 12 | 8 | 4 | 0 | 0 | 0 | 0 | 0 | 0 | 24 |
| Old Xaverians | 12 | 7 | 4 | 0 | 0 | 0 | 0 | 0 | 0 | 23 |
| Liverpool | 12 | 5 | 7 | 0 | 0 | 0 | 0 | 0 | 0 | 15 |
| Maghull | 12 | 4 | 7 | 0 | 0 | 0 | 1 | 0 | 0 | 15 |
| Newton-le-Willows | 12 | 5 | 3 | 0 | 0 | 0 | 0 | 3 | 0 | 14 |
| Sefton Park | 12 | 4 | 8 | 0 | 0 | 0 | 0 | 0 | 0 | 12 |
| Rainford | 12 | 0 | 11 | 0 | 0 | 0 | 1 | 0 | 0 | 3 |

# A season in photographs

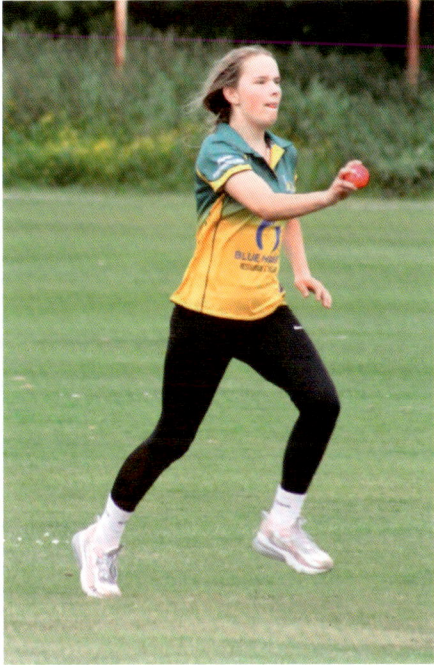

Sarah Curlett bowling
against Wavertree

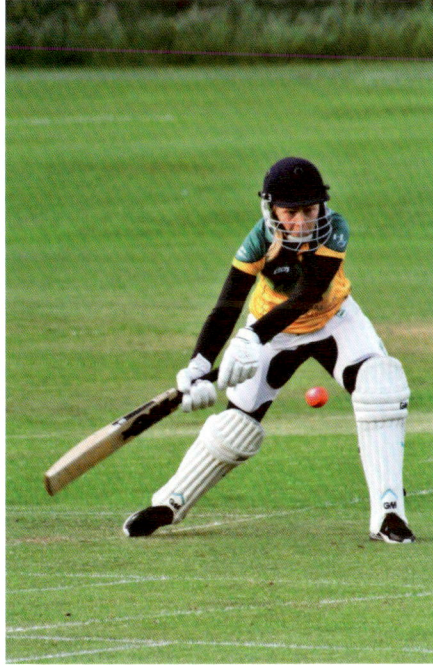

Sue Lowrie on the attack
vs Wavertree

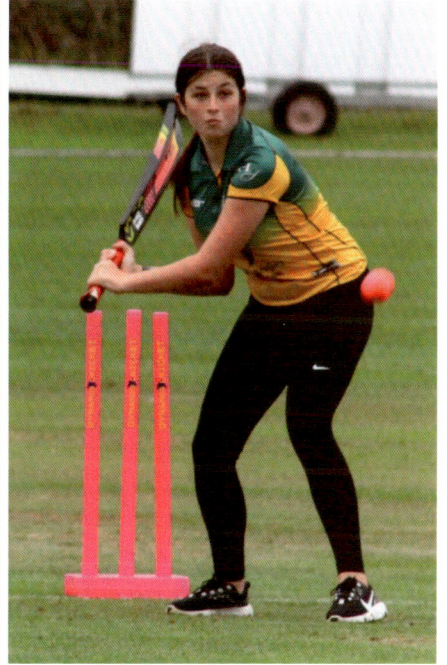

Eyes on the ball—
Lily Murphy vs Southport

Cassie Hopkins in action at home to
Southport

Lucy Brown shows the others how—
vs Southport

Vicky Graham fields on the boundary

Lucy Strettle steams in

**Lucy Strettle and Sarah Curlett were selected for the LDCC team against Lancashire**

**Rainhill vs Bootle B**

**Chloe Gillespie often bowled effectively**

**Planning the next move—vs Bootle B**

**Good running proved crucial—vs Bootle B**

Liv Reilly hitting out vs Bootle B

This could be out...

Susan Rotheram sends the ball to the rope

Bobbie Grant gets in on the act

Julie Foulkes in determined mood vs Bootle B

Jess Bates

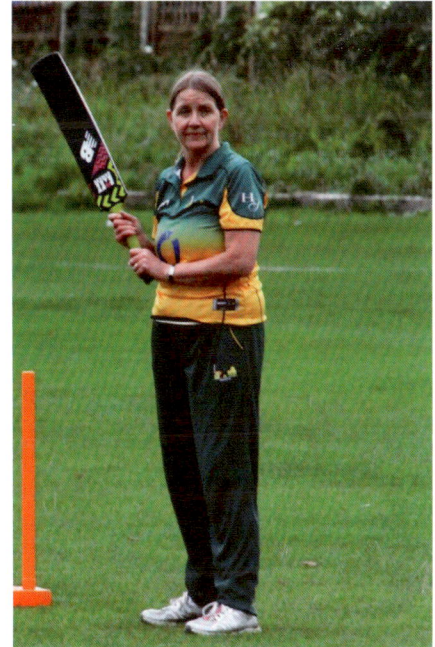
Jayne Curlett

# THE JUNIORS' TALE

Rainhill's junior section had an eventful and, in may respects, highly successful 2021 season.

The club has junior teams in the under 9s, under 11s, under 13s, under 15s and under 18s categories, and in 2021 also had under 10s and under 15s girls' teams. The junior teams have thrived and expanded in recent years, and the addition of dedicated girls' sides has added a welcome new dimension.

Given the number of teams, in telling the story of the juniors it is probably best to take each team in turn and give a brief review of their respective achievements.

## Under 9s

Under the management of John Pearson, the under 9s continued to attract new players and held regular intra-club tournaments in addition to participating in local cricket festivals and tournaments.

The highlight of the season was the Ainsdale CC Tournament in which Rainhill not only fielded two teams but reached two finals. Although they finished on the losing side in their respective action-packed matches, our two sides performed incredibly well against very talented opposition.

Rainhill fielded two sides on account of the large number of players they had available. Ken Rustidge took charge of the A team, while the B team was overseen by John Pearson. The first round was a group stage consisting of ten teams: the top four would go into the semi-finals while teams ranked fifth to eighth would compete in the plate semi-finals. This confused some of the youngsters, but they soon understood when it was explained that the plate event was similar to the Europa League!

Rainhill's B team were in very good shape and soon established themselves as one of the teams to beat. The A team's fortunes were more mixed but they picked up a valuable win against Southport and were unlucky in some of the other games that were very close contests.

Rainhill B were cruising into the semi-finals when they met Rainhill A in the penultimate group match. The encounter between the sides was a close-fought one and the A team pushed their friends all the way but fell just short in their quest for two points. Fortunately the results in the final group matches meant that the A team progressed into the plate semi-finals to meet Formby B, while the B team contested the cup semi-final against Fleetwood Hesketh.

Batting first, Rainhill A produced their best performance of the competition, completing a surprisingly straightforward win over Formby B thanks to some positive batting and some good fielding.  The B team meanwhile had been playing Fleetwood Hesketh, a team that epitomised sportsmanship and fair play. Fleetwood were tough opponents but it was Rainhill B that edged a tense semi-final.

In the plate final Rainhill A posted 226 and, in spite of regularly taking Liverpool wickets, some big-hitting from their opponents meant that the A team had to settle for second place. This they did with great magnanimity. The main final was a hard fought event between the two best teams in the tournament: Rainhill B and Formby A, meaning that a new name on the trophy was guaranteed. There were just nine runs in it, but it was the team from Formby who emerged triumphant. It was a great game and a terrific advertisement for junior cricket.

Some Rainhill players were taking part in their first ever competition and they performed very well.  All involved were a credit to the club and we will surely hear more about them in the future.

**Rainhill under 9s A team (above) and B team (below), Ainsdale Tournament 2021**

**Rainhill under 10s girls**

*Back row: Olivia Clifford, Emily Ashcroft, Maddie Rotheram, Edie Brougham,*
*Alex Lea (team manager), April Jones, Lucy Gibson.*
*Front row: Sarah Lawler, Annabelle Clifford, Erin Jones, Xanthe Page, Lily McCabe, Ruby Murphy*

The under 10s girls' team went the entire season unbeaten. Even more impressive is that they won every one of their 13 matches and that three of their players—April Jones, Maddie Rotheram and Sarah Lawler—were selected for the Lancashire under 11s squad in early 2022 following the successful season.

Like the under 9s, the team did not play in a league but instead took part in local tournament and festivals. They built a formidable reputation for the way in which the approached the game and also made friends with their sportsmanship and fair play.

While Rainhill had some stand-out players, they were also a very good team in all respects and worked hard for each other. Their running between the wickets, for example, was excellent for players so young.

Towards the end of the season Rainhill hosted their own cricket festival, in which the girls participated and—once again—won all of their games against some strong opponents. Teams included Bootle, Liverpool, Northern (two teams), Fleetwood Hesketh Foxes, Sefton Park and Phoenix, all of whom played some fantastic cricket and clearly enjoyed themselves in the process.

While Rainhill's girls finished the season with an amazing record of 13 wins from 13 games, what was perhaps an even greater achievement is the way in which this team has taken shape. Guided by Alex Lea, the girls—most of whom had only recently started playing cricket—have developed a great understanding between themselves and have significantly improved as individuals and as a team. Their talent and potential is obvious and girls' cricket at Rainhill is currently going from strength to strength.

# Photos from the Rainhill Girls' Cricket Festival

**Olivia Clifford**

**April Jones**

**Sarah Lawler**

**Lucy Gibson**

**Xanthe Page**

**Edie Brougham**

**Team talk**

**Maddie Rotheram**

Erin Jones

Action v Sefton Park

Erin Jones and Alex Lea

Star Player: April Jones

Ruby Murphy

Emily Ashcroft

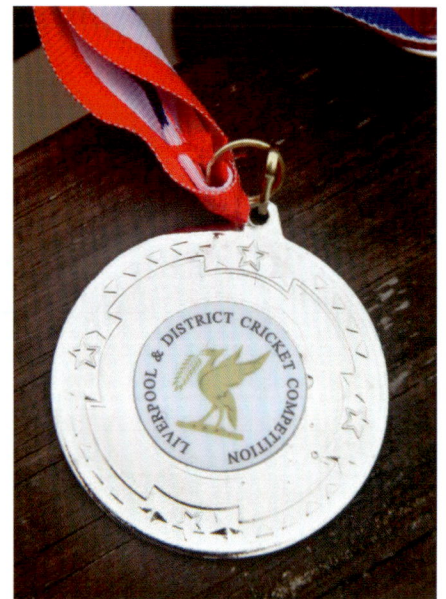
Event medal

## Under 11s

Rainhill's promising under 11s side were placed in a group with two excellent teams in the shape of Liverpool and Ormskirk. Also in the group were Rainford, Bootle and Maghull

It was very much a league within a league with Liverpool and Ormskirk being significantly older, bigger, stronger and more experienced than the newly formed younger squads. However, Rainhill put in some creditable performances over the season and became a visibly stronger and more confident side as the season progressed.

**Rainhill under 11s v Liverpool (h), 27.7.21**

*Back row: Olivia Smedley, Maddie Rotheram, Finnlee Millar, Nathan Lawler, Patrick Reilly, Mattie Ambage.*
*Front row: Ayaan Maheshwari, Charlie Unsworth, Naithan Varghese, Archie Venables, Finlay Venables*

Rainhill gave a positive account of themselves in their opening match against Ormskirk even if the result didn't go their way. They then hosted Liverpool and, although they lost by 42 runs, it was a competitive match with several of the Rainhill youngsters showing their potential.

Rainhill earned a fine 25-run win over Bootle at Victoria Terrace to record their first victory of the season and followed this up with another win away to the same opponents.

Rainhill showed real character and determination in a hard-fought contest as they recorded a famous win over Rainford en route to finishing in fourth place in their group. Improved performances against Ormskirk and Liverpool gave Rainhill under 11s good reason to look back on 2021 as a successful season in which the team became more cohesive and several individuals developed into more intelligent players.

The under 11s have the makings of a very good side and 2021 was a year in which many players demonstrated their aptitude and talent.

Nathan Lawler's batting impressed many opponents, while Finnlee Millar's bowling often created difficulties for even the most accomplished batters at this level. Patrick Reilly, Olivia Smedley and Maddie Rotheram also impressed with the ball. Finlay Venables won the award for most improved player, while the Player of the Year award was shared by Naithan Varghese and Mattie Ambage.

All in all it was a season in which a work in progress took shape and performances became more assured. While Rainhill played well in the games they won, they arguably gave an even better account of themselves in some of the matches in which they were underdogs and fought well against stronger teams. The under 11s will go into the 2022 with justified belief and confidence, and under the excellent new management team of Paul Millar, Ken Rustidge and James Saunders should expect to make further progress.

Rainhill will have two U11 teams in 2022, an A and a B team to try and maximise participation and player progression into hardball cricket.

# Rainhill under 11s in action v Liverpool

**Maddie Rotheram**

**Charlie Unsworth**

**Finlay Venables**

**Archie Venables**

**Olivia Smedley**

**Patrick Reilly**

Finnlee Millar

Nathan Lawler

Mattie Ambage

Naithan Varghese

Ayaan Maheshwari

## LIVERPOOL COMPETITION JUNIOR LEAGUE

## UNDER 11s—GREEN GROUP

### Final Standings

|            | Pl | w  | l | c  | a | lcn | wcn | t | Pen | Pts |
|------------|----|----|---|----|---|-----|-----|---|-----|-----|
| Liverpool  | 14 | 12 | 0 | 1  | 0 | 0   | 1   | 0 | 0   | 39  |
| Ormskirk   | 14 | 7  | 3 | 4  | 0 | 0   | 0   | 0 | 0   | 21  |
| Maghull    | 14 | 3  | 3 | 7  | 0 | 1   | 0   | 0 | 0   | 9   |
| **Rainhill** | **14** | **3** | **6** | **5** | **0** | **0** | **0** | **0** | **0** | **9** |
| Bootle     | 14 | 0  | 9 | 5  | 0 | 0   | 0   | 0 | 0   | 0   |
| Rainford   | 14 | 0  | 4 | 10 | 0 | 0   | 0   | 0 | 0   | 0   |

## Under 13s

Rainhill's promising under 13s team began 2021 with a resounding 146-run win at **Maghull**. Openers Stevie Pennington and Oliver Wallis showed no sign of rustiness and Pennington hit a half-century, which included 9 fours, before retiring unbeaten. Andrew Fairclough scored 31 not out and Ollie Unsworth added 23 as Rainhill reached an astonishing 169-2 from 16 overs.

Maghull never looked capable of chasing down the target, but to their credit were not bowled out in spite of being reduced to 0-2 when Rainhill's opening bowlers, Harry Green and Harry Ball, began their spells with wicket maidens. Jack Tyms took two wickets in successive balls and finished with figures of 3-2 from his two overs. Maghull finished on 24-5 but at least had made something of a game of it and had defied some very good bowling for long spells.

Rainhill then faced tougher opponents at home in the shape of **Widnes**. Knocks of 39 and 27 from Stevie Pennington and Andrew Fairclough respectively gave Rainhill a platform to build on, while Oliver Wallis added an unbeaten contribution of 36 to help his team to a total of 116-3. It was a good score, but Rainhill's bowlers struggled to make much impact against Hassan Malik (38 not out) and Nirek Jaglan (22 not out) and Widnes crossed the finish line with 10 balls to spare.

Away from league action, Rainhill took on **Formby** in the Halliwell Trophy. Having been put into bat by Formby, captain Stevie Pennington (32 not out, retired) and Oliver Wallis (22) put on 53 for the first wicket. Kieran Rose then arrived at the crease and a superb unbeaten innings of 33 from 42 deliveries put Rainhill in a strong position as they closed on 155-2. Formby batted well but couldn't keep up with the required run-rate, with good bowling from Oliver Wallis (1-4), Freddie Foulkes (1-14) and Jack Tyms (0-7) reducing scoring opportunities. Formby reached 131-4 from their 20 overs and Rainhill were into the next round, where they would meet Northern.

Oliver Wallis (32 not out, retired) and Kieran Rose (30 not out, retired) inspired Rainhill to victory over **Bootle** in the next league match. The only wicket to fall in Rainhill's innings was that of Stevie Pennington, who failed to build on recent good form when he was bowled out for 2. Ollie Unsworth added an unbeaten 26 as Rainhill amassed a daunting total of 123-1. Bootle's pursuit began positively but wickets soon began to tumble: Oliver Wallis (2-6), Jack Tyms (2-5) and Mackenzie Henderson (2-7) were the pick of the bowlers, but the team's all-round performance in the field was something to be proud of. Bowling was tight and disciplined throughout. Owen Morrissey bowled 2 overs for just 2 runs, while Leo Brougham bowled 3 overs for just 6. Excellent fielding backed up some superb bowling. .

The win over Bootle propelled Rainhill to the top of the table, but they were brought back down to earth with defeat in the Halliwell Trophy quarter-final to **Northern**. Northern batted first and, while Andrew Fairclough and Jack Tyms took two wickets apiece, some tremendous batting under pressure from Shamal Harave and Seb Rice helped to build a total of 144-7. The task for Rainhill was a tough one but other than Andrew Fairclough (40 not out, retired) no-one was able to score more than 5 and wickets fell frequently. Rainhill were only able to reach 91-9.

Cup exit was followed by a low-scoring four-wicket home victory over **Old Xaverians**. The visitors won the toss and opted to bat, but were bowled out for 48. Rainhill made heavy weather of the chase but, in spite of losing key wickets, were able to navigate their way to 50-6 from 12 overs. Rainhill then recorded another home win, this time against **Wavertree**, by the margin of 52 runs. Rainhill's batting was far more composed with Stevie Pennington (30 not out, retired) and Andrew Fairclough (26) leading the way as the home side marched to 132-6. Wavertree's innings struggled to get going, and their top order was pegged back by some precision bowling from Jack Tyms, Oliver Wallis, Andrew Fairclough and Freddie Foulkes, all of whom took a wicket. Harry Ball (3-8) then ripped through the tail as the visitors struggled to 80 all out.

Rainhill were riding high in the league but so too were **Sefton Park** when the two teams met at the end of June. A close match was anticipated and that's exactly what was played out. Rainhill, batting first, posted 111-6, thanks to the customary strong performance from Stevie Pennington and Ollie Unsworth. In reply, Sefton Park got out of the blocks early and, despite losing an early wicket, Daniel Babu (30 not out, retired) and Tom Spilsbury (33 not out, retired) swung the momentum in their team's favour. Oliver Wallis (2-11) and Kieran Rose (1-7) slowed down the run rate and swept through the middle order but, with three overs left, Sefton Park needed just 11 runs for the win.

Leo Brougham (2-9) bowled Ben Lester for 2 in the 18th over and, with Oliver Wallis collecting a simple caught and bowled in the 19th (Harry Parker going for 0) the ball was thrown to Leo Brougham to bowl the last over with Sefton Park now needing 9 from 6 balls. The field was set tight. A single came from the first ball. Then two dot balls. Then came another wicket as Brougham bowled Seb Wheatcroft for 0! The tension was almost unbearable as Finn Spragg and Luke Rotheram knew that two fours from the two remaining balls would bring victory. The next ball was crashed to the leg-side boundary for 4 and, with the field reset, Leo ran in for the final delivery. Spragg went for the same pull shot and both batters hared off but Harry Ball was perfectly placed to intercept and throw in for Ollie Unsworth to whip off the bails.

The Rainhill players rushed to celebrate a fantastic result and a great ending to a great match. Rainhill cemented themselves in second place and there was a feeling in the team that 2021 might just be their year.

On the following day Rainhill travelled to **Northern** and, confident from the result at Sefton Park, they inflicted a 33-run defeat on their hosts to avenge the Halliwell Trophy loss. Rainhill reached 111-7, with everyone contributing something, before bowling out Northern for 78. Only captain Thomas Gee made double figures, while Rainhill's Aakash Muraleethuran (2-3), Freddie Foulkes (2-5) and Stevie Pennington (1-0) turned in outstanding personal performances.

At the half-way point of the season Rainhill were definite title contenders, but their next four matches were all cancelled (giving neither team any points) and they didn't play another match until August—at home to **Northern**. The previous fine showing against Northern was not repeated and, despite Stevie Pennington's 3-22, the visitors were able to accumulate 126 runs. Rainhill's run chase fizzled out as they were dismissed for a miserable 59.

Rainhill also lost their next two matches—against **Liverpool (Blue)** and **Liverpool (Red)**. In the first of these Rainhill were highly competitive and, chasing 108-4, were perhaps unlucky to fall eight runs short of their target. In the final match of the season Rainhill struggled to 60 all out from 16.5 overs and Liverpool (Red) reached the target comfortably without loss of wickets.

A sixth place finish after having led the league table may seem like a disappointment, and it is true that Rainhill would have wanted to finish the season with something other than a sequence of three successive defeats. However, it should be pointed out that, up to that point, Rainhill had only been beaten once and the four cancelled matches certainly had an impact on the final placings. Rainhill won 6 matches in the league—only the invincible Liverpool (Red) won more—and they recorded some excellent victories against highly talented teams. Looking at the season as a whole the wider picture is one of progress with several strong individual and collective performances. It is clear that several players have the potential to help the team fare even better in 2022.

## LIVERPOOL COMPETITION JUNIOR LEAGUE

### UNDER 13s—BROWN GROUP

#### Final Standings

|  | Pl | w | l | c | a | lcn | wcn | t | Pen | Pts |
|---|---|---|---|---|---|---|---|---|---|---|
| Liverpool (Red) | 14 | 13 | 0 | 0 | 0 | 0 | 1 | 0 | 0 | 42 |
| Liverpool (Blue) | 14 | 6 | 6 | 0 | 0 | 0 | 2 | 0 | 0 | 24 |
| Sefton Park | 14 | 6 | 5 | 0 | 2 | 1 | 1 | 0 | 0 | 23 |
| Northern | 14 | 5 | 6 | 0 | 1 | 0 | 2 | 0 | 0 | 22 |
| Widnes | 14 | 6 | 4 | 3 | 0 | 0 | 1 | 0 | 0 | 21 |
| **Rainhill** | **14** | **6** | **4** | **4** | **0** | **0** | **0** | **0** | **0** | **18** |
| Wavertree | 14 | 5 | 6 | 2 | 1 | 0 | 0 | 0 | 0 | 16 |
| Bootle | 14 | 2 | 5 | 3 | 1 | 1 | 2 | 0 | 0 | 13 |
| Old Xaverians | 14 | 0 | 5 | 2 | 1 | 6 | 0 | 0 | 0 | 1 |
| Maghull | 14 | 0 | 8 | 4 | 0 | 2 | 0 | 0 | 0 | 0 |

## Under 15s

In a season plagued by cancellations and concessions Rainhill's under 15s only played five league matches, winning two and losing the other three.

It was tough on the team, who had five of their matches cancelled and three others conceded by the opposition, but they showed enough in the matches they did play to suggest that they are an improving team with some strong individual players.

After Rainhill's opening match against **Maghull** was cancelled, they travelled to Wadham Road to face **Bootle**. Sam Addy (1-31) struck early to remove Harry Ehlen for 8, but Bootle rallied and Dylan Riley and Luis Craggs both hit half-centuries. Adam Lawler had Matthew Medlicott lbw late in the innings, but the wicket didn't halt the flow of runs and Bootle ended their 20 overs on 161-2. It would have been a tall order to chase down so formidable a target, but Rainhill weren't at the races: Amber Bowie top-scored with 12 as Rainhill slumped to 63-9 and defeat by 98 runs.

After another cancellation (this time against **Liverpool**), Rainhill hosted **Rainford** at Victoria Terrace. Rainhill won the toss and elected to bat, but on a bowler's pitch no-one was able to stay in for long and build a decent innings. For the second successive match Amber Bowie (9 not out) top-scored for Rainhill. Rainford also struggled and were 48-5 before Joe Duffy and Cameron Murtagh took control and guided the visitors to a 5-wicket victory. It was a good performance from Rainhill with the ball, with Sam Addy (2-7), Motsim Khan (1-5), Thomas Lewis (1-7) and Ned Brougham (1-10) all stifling the batsmen and taking valuable wickets.

The next two scheduled league matches, against **Old Xaverians** and **Maghull**, were conceded by the opposition. Rainhill then found themselves in cup action, against **Sefton Park** in the Davies Shield. After a disappointing start after which Rainhill found themselves on 24-4, Stevie Pennington (14) and Ollie Unsworth (16) attempted to engineer something of a comeback. It wasn't quite enough, but the score of 71-7 at least gave Rainhill something to bowl at.

Sefton Park lost early wickets too as Sam Addy (2-14) struck twice within the space of three deliveries. Unfortunately Rainhill were unable to make any further breakthrough and Sefton Park eased to 72-2 with six overs remaining.

Rainhill were without a win when they met **Liverpool**. Always a great place to play cricket, Rainhill responded to their surroundings and raised their game against a very good Liverpool team. The hosts batted first and were pleased with their 107-3, with Ashar Sohail (1-11), Sam Addy (1-12) and a run out accounting for the three Liverpool wickets. Openers Kieran Rose (23 not out) and Motsim Khan (33 not out, retired) built a solid platform before two late wickets meant the game hung in the balance. Rose and Ashar Sohail held their nerve in the final over and Sohail hit the winning boundary with just two balls to spare. It had been that close!

The win was a tonic for Rainhill and provided a welcome boost of confidence prior to the match against **Rainford**. Rainhill's bowlers were impressive as they restricted their opponents to 82-5;

special mention should go to Sam Addy (2-10), Adam Lawler (1-10) and Gianni Albanese (1-13). Rainhill's Motsim Khan (33) and Stevie Pennington (18) got off to a fantastic start but, once they were out, the middle order collapsed and despite the efforts of Amber Bowie and Thomas Lewis they were unable to find the necessary runs as time ran out. Rainhill finished agonisingly short of their target on 76-7.

However disappointing the defeat, the performance gave reasons to feel positive. Due to a string of matches being either cancelled or conceded, the under 15s' final match of 2021 was at home to **Maghull**. Rainhill put Maghull in to bat, and the visitors responded by making a meritorious 124-7. Sam Addy once again impressed, taking 3-28, but Maghull would have felt that they had posted a more than adequate target.

In their best batting performance of the year, Rainhill successfully chased down the required score—although it went down to the final ball! An unbeaten half-century from Sam Addy and solid knocks from Stevie Pennington (17), Sarah Curlett (15) and Gianni Albanese (14 not out) all proved vital and it was Albanese who struck the winning runs to ensure Rainhill's second league victory of the season—and a third place league finish.

The under 15s are a team in transition but they improved as the season progressed. A lot of markers were laid down and there were sufficient indications that the team is beginning to "gel" and perform well under pressure. Stevie Pennington, Sam Addy, Motsim Khan and Ollie Unsworth can compete with the best at this level and will hopefully be able to continue their form into the new season. There is every reason to believe that 2022 will be a good year for Rainhill's under 15s.

**Thomas Lewis**

**LIVERPOOL COMPETITION JUNIOR LEAGUE**

**UNDER 15s—YELLOW DEVELOPMENT GROUP**

**Final Standings**

|  | Pl | w | l | c | a | lcn | wcn | t | Pen | Pts |
|---|---|---|---|---|---|---|---|---|---|---|
| Bootle | 14 | 4 | 1 | 4 | 1 | 0 | 4 | 0 | 0 | 25 |
| Liverpool | 12 | 3 | 1 | 6 | 0 | 0 | 2 | 0 | 0 | 15 |
| **Rainhill** | **13** | **2** | **3** | **5** | **0** | **0** | **3** | **0** | **0** | **15** |
| Rainford | 13 | 2 | 3 | 7 | 1 | 0 | 0 | 0 | 0 | 7 |
| Maghull | 14 | 0 | 3 | 10 | 0 | 1 | 0 | 0 | 0 | 0 |
| Old Xaverians | 14 | 0 | 0 | 6 | 0 | 8 | 0 | 0 | 0 | 0 |

## Under 15s girls

Rainhill's under 15s girls team started 2021 with an ECB Club T20 Cup match against **Wavertree**. Wavertree batted first and an unbeaten 51 from Aoife Donahue helped them to a total of 132-3 from their 20 overs. Rainhill found the going tough against an experienced bowling attack but to their credit kept on battling to close their innings on 44-7.

The girls had only one previous season in league competition—in 2020—when they lost all of their matches. For a relatively new team the ambition for 2021 was to become more competitive and to further develop the young players, many of whom had already shown promise.

In 2021 Rainhill's girls participated in the Super 8s Hardball League. As the name suggest, this is an 8 per side competition. Each innings lasts for 16 overs as batters play in pairs for four overs at a time. Teams start with a net score of 200. Runs scored are added to that total while each wicket lost results in five runs being deducted.

Rainhill's first match of the season was at Sandy Lane against **Hightown St Mary's**. Rainhill batted first and reached 65-8, giving them a net score of 225. Rainhill bowled well to limit Hightown to 62-4 from their 16 overs but unfortunately Rainhill lost out on account of the wickets lost. Hightown's net score of 242 was enough to get them off to a winning start, while Rainhill knew they had pushed their opponents hard and had given a good account of themselves.

Rainhill's next game was against **Upton**. It was once again a close run contest and, as in the Wavertree match, the number of wickets lost during Rainhill's innings proved crucial. Upton made 87-3 (net score 272) while Rainhill progressed to 81-6 (net score 251). Two matches and two defeats may not look brilliant on paper but in both games Rainhill were competitive and played positively throughout.

The next match was a friendly against fellow Super 8s side **Tarleton**. Lucy Brown (15), Lucy Strettle (14) and Paris Cook (10) showed real purpose as they sought to score quickly. Brown was particularly impressive and never looked in any real trouble against some pretty accurate bowling. Unfortunately for Rainhill, they lost seven wickets as they scored 66 runs from their 16 overs, giving them a net score of 231. In reply Tarleton were only able to accumulate 46 runs but as Rainhill were only able to take one wicket the net score of 241 was enough to give them a ten-run victory.

**Lucy Brown**

Back in league action against **Wavertree**, Rainhill posted a total of 58-5. Amber Bowie and Katie Roberts starred with the bat as Rainhill recorded a net score of 233. It never looked like enough against a strong Wavertree team but Rainhill bowled well, with Chloe Gillespie (1-3), Olivia Smedley (1-4) and Amber Bowie (1-12) all taking wickets and giving Rainhill hope until Wavertree's last pairing of Jasmine Dunn and Cassie Kennedy-Nation added 19 runs to make sure of the win.

Rainhill's final scheduled game against **Tarleton** was cancelled—somewhat unfortunately as it would have provided an opportunity for both teams to record their first league win of the season. The girls may have finished the season winless but performances were much improved and the team became a more cohesive unit.

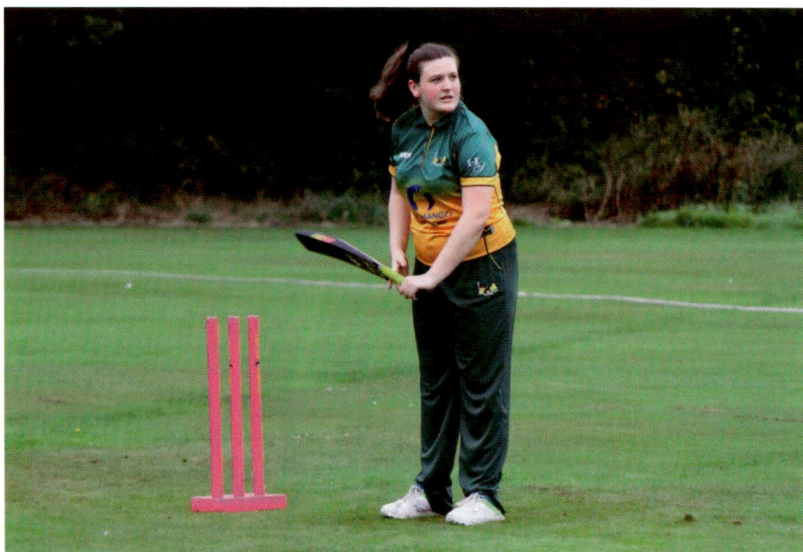

**Katie Roberts**

At the end of season awards, coach Mike Rotheram gave the bowling award to "two exceptional young bowlers", Amber Bowie and Chloe Gillespie. The batting award went to Lily Murphy, of whom Rotheram said "She only started playing the game two years ago. She hits the ball super hard, very athletic and likes to speak in the field." The players' player of the year was Katie Roberts, who "led the team brilliantly well throughout the year, captained the team, led from the front in all aspects. She bats, bowls, fields and runs people out for fun."

Several of the under 15s girls squad also featured in games for the women's hardball and softball teams in 2021. It's clear there is a talented group of players in this team and, as they become more experienced and make further progress in 2022, they will become more competitive still.

To be where they are after just two years is a success story in itself. The team is now firmly established and a core part of Rainhill Cricket Club. The under 15s girls' side is an ongoing work in progress but the vision to develop girls' cricket and has been integral to a change of culture at the club. The dedication of the players and coach, with the support of the committee, will help drive further growth and transformation as participation increases.

**LIVERPOOL COMPETITION WOMEN AND GIRLS LEAGUE**

**GIRLS UNDER 15s SUPER 8s HARDBALL LEAGUE**

**Final Standings**

|  | Pl | w | l | c | a | lcn | wcn | t | Pen | Pts |
|---|---|---|---|---|---|---|---|---|---|---|
| Wavertree | 4 | 3 | 0 | 0 | 1 | 0 | 0 | 0 | 0 | 10 |
| Upton | 4 | 2 | 1 | 0 | 1 | 0 | 0 | 0 | 0 | 7 |
| Hightown St Mary's | 4 | 2 | 2 | 0 | 0 | 0 | 0 | 0 | 0 | 6 |
| Tarleton | 4 | 0 | 1 | 1 | 2 | 0 | 0 | 0 | 0 | 3 |
| **Rainhill** | **4** | **0** | **3** | **1** | **0** | **0** | **0** | **0** | **0** | **1** |

## Under 18s

Under the management of Paul Duffy the under 18 were unbeaten in 2021—the only team other than the under 10s girls to achieve this.

Admittedly the under 18s played fewer matches but, given the quality of their opponents, finishing in top spot in their league was a great accomplishment and underlines just how good a unit they have become.

The under 18s started their season against **Northern**. James Clarke and Jack Ellis shared an opening

**Rainhill under 18s v Ormskirk, 28.6.21**

partnership of 90, which was only ended when Clarke played a ball from Jack Bovill to Hugh Hodkinson. Clarke had looked in excellent form, taking only 43 balls to score his 65—an innings that included 9 fours and 2 sixes. Ellis's more patient innings of 38 from 43 deliveries was ended when he was bowled by Bovill but Owen Groom (42 not out) and Luis Duffy (12 not out) kept the runs flowing and took the score on to 167-2.

Against some determined Rainhill bowling and excellent fielding, several Northern players made positive starts but were unable to score at the rate required. As they tried to accelerate wickets inevitably fell and Northern slipped from 70-1 to 124-7. Owen Groom (2-4) and Ethan Powell (2-16) blew away the middle order as Rainhill got off to a winning start.

With the match at New Brighton cancelled, Rainhill's next match was a home game against **Ormskirk**. The visitors won the toss and batted first but, aside from opener Alex McNally, their

**Luis Duffy**

strong batting line-up had little answer to the questions posed by Rainhill's bowlers. As wickets fell regularly McNally single-handedly defied Rainhill and hit a fluent—and highly entertaining—92 from just 57 balls. He eventually succumbed to Jack Lowrie (2-10) just eight runs short of what would have been a brilliant century and his innings had helped Ormskirk to a pretty decent score of 142-7. Aside from McNally only Nathan Brighouse (15) had managed to reach double figures but, in spite of that, Rainhill had been set a challenging target.

Rainhill opener Luis Duffy was out to the second ball of the innings, caught by Sam Mitchell. However, Jack Ellis (73 not out) and Owen Groom (49 not out) responded positively to the setback and played some superb shots to all areas of the ground as they saw Rainhill to 144-1 with 2.5 overs remaining. The comprehensive nature of the victory against a very good Ormskirk side confirmed that Rainhill were definitely a team to watch in 2021.

The next match for the under 18s was away to **Rainford**, Rainhill put in a fantastic performance in the field to restrict the hosts to 96-5. James Clarke trapped Luke Evans lbw for 5 before running out fellow opener Matthew Noble for 12. Rainford recovered from 23-2 but they found scoring difficult and the target seemed straightforward enough for Rainhill.

Rainhill started poorly as openers Clarke and Jack Ellis were soon back in the pavilion with the score on 17-2. However, Ethan Powell (27 not out), Luis Duffy (21) and Oliver Powell (17) were able to turn the game around and ensured Rainhill were home with five balls to spare. Rainford had put up a determined fight but once again Rainhill's under 18s had responded positively and played themselves out of a difficult situation.

The win at Rainford was to prove the final game of the season for the under 18s due to further matches being cancelled. It was an unsatisfactory way to finish the year but the under 18s will look back on the games they did play in 2021 and reflect on a job well done. None of the matches were straightforward and they were all won against good sides who created difficulties for Rainhill—difficulties that Rainhill were able to overcome. The depth of character in the squad was self-evident and several of the players are well-placed to make their mark in senior cricket (indeed, some already have done so).

**James Clarke**

## LIVERPOOL COMPETITION JUNIOR LEAGUE

### UNDER 18s—GREEN GROUP

#### Final Standings

|  | Pl | w | l | c | a | lcn | wcn | t | Pen | Pts |
|---|---|---|---|---|---|---|---|---|---|---|
| **Rainhill** | **6** | **3** | **0** | **3** | **0** | **0** | **0** | **0** | **0** | **9** |
| Ormskirk | 6 | 1 | 1 | 3 | 1 | 0 | 0 | 0 | 0 | 4 |
| Rainford | 6 | 1 | 1 | 3 | 1 | 0 | 0 | 0 | 0 | 4 |
| New Brighton | 6 | 1 | 0 | 5 | 0 | 0 | 0 | 0 | 0 | 3 |
| Northern | 6 | 0 | 3 | 2 | 1 | 0 | 0 | 0 | 0 | 1 |
| Old Xaverians | 6 | 0 | 1 | 4 | 1 | 0 | 0 | 0 | 0 | 1 |

**Rainhill LMS team v Earlestown Griffins (a), 25.8.21**

*Back row: Neil Robinson, Asif Junaid, David Pennington, Matt Pennington, Paul Millar (c)*
*Front row: Ethan Powell, Lucy Strettle, Thomas Lewis*

Last Man Stands (LMS) is the world's largest amateur cricket league, and this unique format of cricket has players in the UK, India, Pakistan, Australia, New Zealand, Barbados and South Africa - as well as less traditional homes of cricket such as Austria, the USA, Argentina, China, Bhutan, Finland, Rwanda and even the tiny island of St Helena!

A global phenomenon, LMS is actually quite simple. It is an 8 a-side, 2 hour long T20 game with Double Play and Steal rules. It is a form of cricket designed for amateur cricket of all abilities while also giving opportunities to all to excel. It is generally seen as "a bit of fun" allowing club players from all teams to take part in some extra midweek games, but participating teams can take part in the LMS World Cup or LMS Super Series events.

Rainhill's LMS team have been successful in recent years and, in 2020, were the Warrington and District LMS champions. In 2021 the team, captained by Jack Lowrie, sought to defend its title.

**Jack Lowrie**

The Warrington and District Premiership was made up of 6 teams in 2021, with each playing the others three times. Rainhill's LMS season kicked off with a game against **Sutton St Helens** which was won by 6 wickets. Sutton made 127-4, restricted by some excellent bowling from Joe Harvey (2-11) and David Pennington (1-12). Sam Williamson hit an unbeaten 54 from 34 deliveries as Rainhill reached their target with five overs to spare.

**David Pennington bowling against Earlestown Griffins**

Rainhill also won their next two matches, against **Travellers' Tigers** and **King's Club**, by eight runs and two wickets respectively. A half century from Jack Ellis and a quickfire 45 from Paul Valentine made the difference against Tigers. Unfortunately, after three successive victories Rainhill fell to a 24-run defeat against **Earlestown Griffins** despite the efforts of Simon Brown (35) and Jack Lowrie (24) with the bat.

Rainhill bounced back from the loss and would go another nine games before again tasting defeat. After comfortably seeing off **Sutton St Helens** once again, Jack Lowrie's team recorded a five-wicket win over **Travellers' Tigers** thanks to Jack Ellis's knock of 53 from 28 deliveries. Rainhill then met **Earlestown Raiders** who batted well but had no answer to the aggression of Owen Groom and Jack Ellis, both of whom hit unbeaten half-centuries.

Aside from the blip against Earlestown Griffins, the season so far had gone very well for Rainhill. It was to get better with another straightforward win over **King's Club**—including, once again, half-centuries for Groom and Ellis—before a comprehensive victory over **Griffins** to avenge their previous defeat. Astonishingly, Groom and Ellis both hit fifties for a third successive match.

In a low-scoring match against **Sutton St Helens** the duo were unable to extend this feat, but Rainhill continued their impressive form with a straightforward 7-wicket win. Jack Lowrie (2-16) and Luis Duffy (2-9) helped Rainhill to a 4-wicket win over Travellers' Tigers, while the next game—against **Earlestown Raiders**—proved a very one-sided affair. After bowling Raiders out for 100, Luis Duffy (51 not out) and Jack Ellis (47 not out) had little trouble knocking off the required runs in just 12 overs.

After eight successive wins Rainhill came unstuck against **King's Club**, losing by just 1 run. In a fantastic contest King's Club batted first and made 150-3, with Ian Hall impressing with an unbeaten 52. Rainhill scored quickly in pursuit of the target but also lost crucial wickets. The game went down to the final ball but Rainhill were unable to pull off what would have been an incredible victory, leaving King's Club the victors by the narrowest of margins.

In the final two matches a half-century for Sam Williamson helped his team to a 57-run win over **Earlestown Raiders** to secure the league title, while some excellent batting from Neil Robinson (51 not out) and Ethan Powell (52 not out) earned a great win against second-placed **Earlestown Griffins**. Rainhill had retained the championship and had done it playing positively and adventurously. Whether they will manage to achieve three successive titles remains to be seen, but new LMS captain Neil Robinson will certainly be looking to establish Rainhill as the best LMS team in the local area.

**Ethan Powell**

# THE VOLUNTEERS' TALE

**Volunteers make great things happen**

Like all cricket clubs, Rainhill CC is dependent on the dedication and efforts of a fantastic team of volunteers, and it would be remiss to overlook them when telling the story of the club's 150th anniversary season. Without the work of our volunteers there would be no pitch to play on, no-one to keep score, no umpires for most teams, no coaches and no-one to deal with the day-to-day management of running the club.

The committee in 2021 consisted of John Rotheram (Chairman for the 21st consecutive year), Peter Mercer (President and Secretary), John Pearson (Treasurer), Mike Rotheram (Club Captain), Craig Brougham (Safeguarding Officer), Andrew Page (Communications Officer) and team captains. The contributions these people made, both individually and collectively, was immense. John Pearson did significant work in helping the club to adopt new practices during the pandemic. Many committee members carried out multiple roles at the club.

Ross Higham (pictured), Mike Rotheram and Ben Edmundson took on additional responsibilities for grounds work in a season when the club did not have a dedicated groundsperson, Tom McKeown and John Veacock carried out valuable work on the outfield and machinery. Alan Clarke oversaw the general tidying up of the ground and maintained the hanging baskets. Richard Appleton should also be mentioned for his frequent help in keeping the ground looking tidy.

**Ross Higham**

A cricket club needs its coaches and in this respect Rainhill were very fortunate to have a terrific coaching team. The club would like to thank, in no particular order, the efforts of team managers Alex Lea, John Pearson, Ian Addy, Paul Duffy, Darren Tyms, John Ball, Adam Friar, Andy Roberts and Mike Rotheram and coaches Lucy Strettle, Sarah Curlett, Paul Millar, Ken Rustidge, Andrew Page and Peter Mercer. All of them should be proud of the way in which they have encouraged and supported people—especially young people—to enjoy cricket and become better players. It's worth pointing out that they are all DBS checked, as are most of our volunteers.

Rainhill Cricket Club is privileged to have an outstanding media team, and we like to think it is the best in our local area. Central to this is the club's website, which was designed and created by Andrew and Anna Page in early 2021. Anna's technical knowledge was central to creating a website that did everything the club wanted it to, while Andrew's regular updates (including detailed and often entertaining match reports) and professional quality photographs were appreciated not only by Rainhill players and supporters but by those of many other clubs. Andrew also began producing videos for the club in 2021, while Jack Lowrie took over production of matchday programme. Jack expanded the programme, produced it in both hard and digital forms and used his graphic design skills to create an altogether more impacting cover and layout. It's fair to say that the media team has had a significant impact on improving communications and the way the club is seen more widely.

Rainhill's scorers, Andrew Finney and David Crossley, have over ninety years of service between them. Andrew marked a half-century as Rainhill's first team scorer this season — something that was celebrated at the annual awards event — while David has 43 years under his belt and is looking forward to many more. Craig Brougham scored for some of the junior teams, as occasionally did several other volunteers. The club (and especially those players obsessed with their statistics and averages) is grateful to all scorers for the dedicated service they give.

**Andrew Finney**

Where would we be without umpires? John Veacock (2nd team umpire, who retired at the end of the season after 10 years), Matt Yorke (3rd team) and John Pearson (who umpired several games, including under-18s) were outstanding and performed their duties to a very high standard. The club is proud to have umpires that are not only widely respected but also liked by players of all clubs.

Mike Bradley's efforts on the fundraising front, particularly with ball sponsorship and organising the golf day, were magnificent. It was also volunteers who were responsible for the organisation of the successful 150th Anniversary Gala, but that is another tale...

Ultimately most people associated with the club are volunteers and there are very many more than we have mentioned here: the parents who have helped with All-Stars or who stepped in as scorer at a junior match, the players who tidied the nets area, the people who go the extra mile to do the routine things that nobody really thinks about. They're all central to what happens at Rainhill Cricket Club and to what we are as a club. We've always been about people and we're very grateful for the people we have.

# THE UMPIRE'S TALE

**"That was definitely hitting middle stump!"**

Matt Yorke's involvement with Rainhill Cricket Club started in 2019, when he took part in a charity match in aid of the Campaign Against Living Miserably (CALM) towards the end of the season. Since then he has progressed into a regular umpire and in 2021 took charge on several games involving either the 3rd XI or the Sunday team.

At a time when it's proving difficult to attract new umpires, his willingness to don the white coat and officiate in matches has been of enormous benefit to the club. But what makes him do it? And, most importantly, does he enjoy it?

Yorke says "I came to Rainhill for the charity game and stayed here. I had never played cricket before but thought I would give it a go. I really enjoyed it, so the following year I joined the Sunday team. In the games I played in I never did well with my batting as I always used to find a fielder and so my time was playing was limited.

"We never had an umpire in those games. It was the players who would do this, and I really enjoyed this part as you get a great view of the game and it was good to be able to help the team, as many players definitely did not like doing it!

"I enjoy being an umpire as it is the best seat in the house. You get to see some great bowling and batting. I feel I have a consistent approach which is all the teams can ask for, as umpires are not going to get everything right, but as long as we are consistent it helps towards a good game."

The 2021 season saw him dedicate his time exclusively to umpiring. He explains: "Last season I only umpired and I was involved in the majority of the games for which I was available. Unfortunately there was some time when I was away and also when I had surgery, but I felt I had a good run and gained a lot of experience. I feel this has made me a better umpire and given me a deeper understanding on the game.

"For 2022 I am on a league panel, which I feel will only help me become better and help my overall ability as an umpire."

Reflecting on the Rainhill CC's anniversary season, Yorke feels proud to be part of a club that is so deeply rooted in the community. "For the club to get to 150 years I think is a fantastic achievement. There has been so much progress in the few years I have been involved. It is great for the club to have been in the community for so long, and the Gala taking place last year was a good way for the community to get a look at what the club is doing.

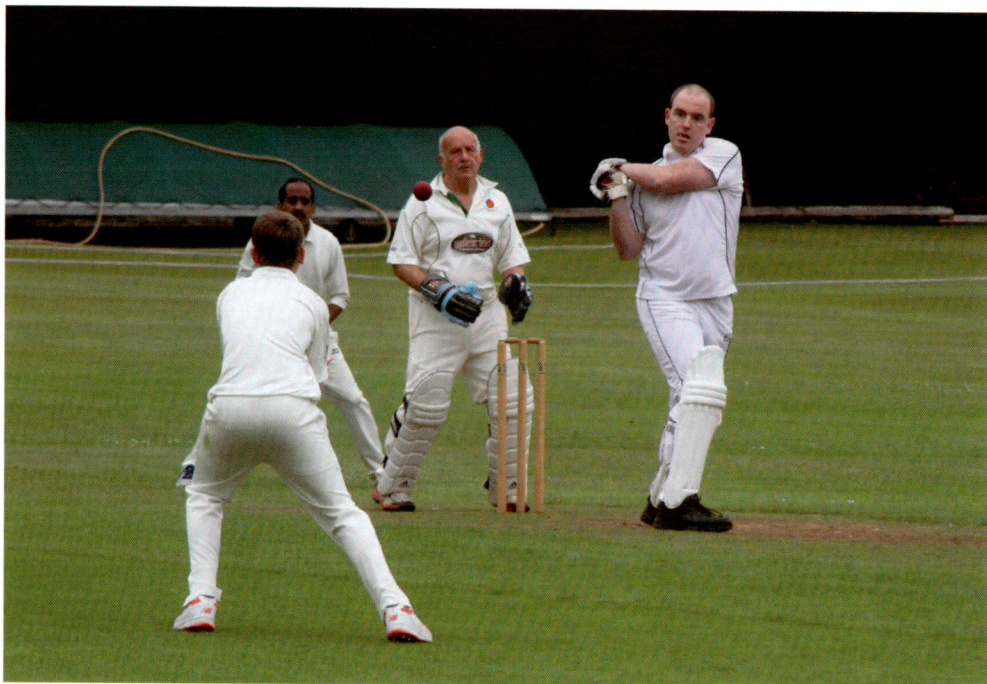

**Matt Yorke playing in the CALM match, 2019**

"I was solely involved with the Sunday team when I first joined, and then last year helped out with the 3rd team, and this year we even have a 4th team due to the number of players at the club expanding. This can only stand the club in good stead going forward as we are able to offer all levels of cricket. The club has had a massive push on women's cricket which is good, as cricket is seen as a men's game. It's also been very good, as an umpire, to see women playing for the men's teams, which can only be good for the game—and the club—going forward."

In many respects Matt Yorke is the personification of Rainhill Cricket Club's core values. After initially becoming involved in a community event focused on increasing mental health awareness, he discovered that he enjoyed cricket and the welcoming environment provided at Rainhill. This in turn led him to dedicate his time and energies towards helping others enjoy the game

Umpires don't make headlines. Their names do not appear on Play Cricket other than as a footnote. No-one makes a record of the hours they spend in the middle. It's not a glamorous role and is often an unloved position, but it is a vital one. Yorke—and Rainhill's other umpires, John Veacock (who retired at the end of the season, after ten years' service) and John Pearson—did so much in 2021 that not only ensured fair oversight of matches but enhanced the reputation of the club. And for that we should all be grateful.

When I was 8 or 9 years old I played cricket in the avenue. It was very narrow and you had to play straight otherwise you would hit the ball into neighbours' gardens for six and OUT! However, Thursday evenings and Saturdays were spent at Granddad's farm. This was much better for cricket as the farmyard was square, although a well-timed pull shot was likely to smash one of the barn's army of small windows, which was not an event that matched up with Granddad's idea of entertainment.

Playing in the farmyard I learned that shots to leg were best played on or very near the ground. Not only were the barn windows best avoided, but anything played above them was likely to end up on the roof – involving getting a big ladder to retrieve the ball – and was 6 and OUT. Straight drives were likely to end up in the vegetable and fruit farm garden, a source of income at the market stall and therefore not to be trampled underfoot or dislodged during searches for lost balls. Balls going into the fruit and vegetables were not only unpopular with Granddad: we didn't enjoy losing so much valuable cricket time!

**Joe Crossley**

When into our teens, we graduated to the nearby level field adjacent to the farm drive, which formed the side boundary, encouraging late and square cuts and cover drives. Consall Lane was there to encourage on/off and straight drives, while our experience of Avenue and farmyard cricket had already got us out of the habit of hitting across the line and towards the expanse of the 5-acre top field!

It can be concluded that a suitable location, such as an avenue or play street, strongly encourages playing straight, especially when off and leg side shots are not only likely to result on getting out but risk the ire of neighbours.

Later, as a schoolboy cricketer, I was strongly influenced by the Leek Cricket Club player who – as a teacher – supposedly coached the school's teams. When I netted he stood by the net and regularly annoyed me by coughing or loudly clearing his throat after nearly every ball, without ever offering a word of advice or encouragement! My response was to attack every ball, come what may – the result was I batted at number 5 where I would batter the tiring opening bowlers or, if they had been replaced by slower medium-pace bowlers, do the same or even more so!

The captain of the North Staffordshire League 2nd XI had seen me playing straight in the nets at Ashcombe Park Cricket Club and soon had me opening the batting on Saturdays. I was given the specific instruction of batting for as long as possible to see off the opening bowlers. As captain (and fellow opener who scored freely) he was adamant that runs were not my priority. I recall two occasions when I finished on 27 and 24 not out, batting with a number 10 and 11, to gain a win and a draw respectively! There was no T20 cricket in those days, so we were encouraged to develop patience and treat every ball on its merits.

## Why I joined the Friendly team

When I initially came to Rainhill I played for the 1st XI, but I found it too serious. I did reasonably well but I felt there was too much pressure at that level and so, in 1977, I began playing for what was then called the Friendly team.

Rainhill's friendly team was new at the time and its first captain was Derek Knight. Derek was a 1st XI batsman who batted down the order but had scored centuries against decent teams and was a champion of the values of friendly cricket. He also had all the attributes of a good captain and the friendly team gave everyone the opportunity to have a go at whatever they wanted. The underpinning principle was that everyone should have an enjoyable game of cricket—win, lose or draw.

Derek asked me to open the batting with him or with whoever else fancied opening up. There were never any recriminations or negative criticisms and Derek was always encouraging and sympathetic towards others' ill-fortunes. Also playing for us in the early days was Jack Williams, a former 1st XI opening bowler and a pretty fast one—he was equally relaxed and never downcast, not even in games such as one at Winton in the late 1970s.

The Winton match is best remembered for the excellent exercise we had in the field as our opponents batted first and amassed 257-2. In the main, our contributions were restricted to retrieving the ball from surrounding fields. The ball also smashed the windscreen of Peter Woods' car, which meant that he actually kept to the speed limit on the M62 on the journey home. Andrew Birkett—at the time a 1st XI opening bowler with his younger brother Dave—took two early wickets. Chasing a formidable target we were all out for 35 and so only lost by 222 runs—even the presence of 1st XI opening batsman Peter Woods did not give scorer David Crossley much work to do! All the same, we all enjoyed the sunny afternoon. The joy of playing was enough—and this has always been what the friendly/Sunday team has been about.

## Memorable matches

The 150th anniversary seems an appropriate moment to look back over the Sunday team's most memorable matches. One of these was against **Northern** in 2007 when a friend of regular batsman Sarfraz Khan— Ijaz Faqih—made an appearance for us. Ijaz had played 5 Tests and 27 One Day Internationals for Pakistan during the 1980s and had scored 6338 First Class runs (at an average of 32.74) and taken 582 wickets (average 23.54). Ijaz is one of only three Rainhill players to have played Test cricket—the others are Bangladesh's Mohammad Ashraful and New Zealand's Ian Butler.

**Ijaz Faqih**

We won the toss and asked Northern to bat. They always fielded a strong batting side and I felt that, batting second, we may at least have the chance of playing out an honourable draw. As captain I asked Ijaz if he would like to open the bowling but he wouldn't hear of it, saying that the regular bowlers should open. Mark Leather took 5-22 and when Ijaz finally got the opportunity he was let down by some of the worst fielding ever! Six dropped catches meant that he finished with less than flattering figures of 1-48 in spite of some superb bowling. We naturally apologised for the poor fielding, but Ijaz shrugged and said "it's just one of those days!"

Ijaz opened the batting with our own Pakistani star, Pankach Lal. Ijaz stroked his way effortlessly to 64 from 37 balls before being stumped, while Pankach hit 37 from 31 to get

Rainhill off to a flying start, moving to 89-1 off 12 overs. Unfortunately, once they were out no-one else was able to score freely, but the team did commendably well to hold out for a draw. It was quite surreal to see a former Test player turning out for Rainhill's Sunday XI and those of us fortunate to have played with him will never forget the occasion!

Another memorable game took place the following season against **Liverpool**. We closed our innings on 228-3, thanks to a splendid knock of 101 not out from Ashok Bohra and a sublime innings of 82 from Robert Hanson. It was a great partnership with Bohra and Hanson putting on 140 for the third wicket. Liverpool managed to cling on for the draw, finishing on 175-7, but it had been a great day for Rainhill's batting.

The return match against **Liverpool** in the same season was also memorable, albeit for different reasons. This Liverpool were dismissed for 188 as Daniel Spreckley took 6-37. Chasing a moderate total, Rainhill were in trouble at 135-7 but Andrew Birkett—coming in at number 8—played a match-winning innings of 45 not out. It was a classically patient innings in which Andrew waited for poor balls to ruthlessly dispatch to the boundary. It wasn't plain sailing though, especially when the ninth wicket fell with the score on 171 and Rainhill needing 18 runs for the win. Andrew's resistance combined with a resilient 8 not out from number 11 Ian Birch gave Rainhill a remarkable victory by the narrowest of margins.

Matches are not always memorable because of their outcome. I recall a match at **Sale** in the 1990s which was Andrew Ford's first senior game. I think he was 11 at the time, which was permitted back then. The opposition, seeing such a diminutive figure coming in at number 4 bowled him a nice easy half-volley first ball—which he cover drove for four! The bowler had been moving the ball about a bit and had until that point been very effective, but being smashed to the boundary by an 11 year-old clearly affected his confidence. Andrew plundered another 31 runs—quite an achievement in his first ever senior match.

In another match against **Sale**, Andrew Birkett opened the batting for us after Sale had amassed a total over 200. We seldom beat Sale and they had a tendency to put out a very strong top order—usually one of their batsmen would score a century. Andrew played his usual sensible, patient innings, expertly picking out the right balls to attack. We weren't able to chase down the target but going into the final over we needed to bat out for the draw. I was there with him at the end. It came down to the final ball and Andrew was determined to run three. We'd run two and I could see the third was definitely not on, so I refused. We had saved the game but he was furious! It turned out he'd calculated that he'd finished on 99 not out and so was unhappy at missing out on a century. Fortunately for him scorer David Crossley was able to show him that he had, in fact, miscounted and the two runs were sufficient to reach his well-deserved century.

We played another match in the palatial surroundings of Arley Hall—one of the advantages of friendly cricket is visits to unusual places. I think the opposition was **Midland Bank**. The ground is a Victorian

**The Pavilion at Arley Hall (Photo: Jeff Buck)**

one with a Victorian facility—with no electricity, gas or water... but a very good tea! It had rained so much before the match that the outfield was saturated: at one point I attempted to stop the ball but inadvertently stood on it, after which it disappeared into the ground. Also, an adjoining field had a number of cows in it and a requisite number of cowpats. Inevitably the ball found these on several occasions and naturally there was great reluctance to retrieve the ball. I can't remember anything about the scores but it was memorable for the various other things that sometimes happen in Sunday cricket.

The last time we played **Liverpool** at Aigburth we used the First Class dressing rooms. We had reinforcements in the shape of David Birkett, who took two wickets, but two Liverpool batsmen scored centuries and the best we could hope for was to play for a draw. It's not often Sunday XI players have the opportunity to perform at a First Class ground, so the venue naturally inspires you to do your best. I'd been reading before the game of the records that had been set at Aigburth and some of the

**Aigburth, home of Liverpool CC**

great players of the past who had appeared there—including Archie McLaren, the Lancashire batsman who in 1895 became the first player to record a quadruple-hundred with 424 against Somerset. So I was determined to do well! I batted for over an hour for 9 not out to secure a draw! I was batting at number 7 and Liverpool brought back the opening bowler to finish off the tail. He decided to "give me the treatment" and bowled me a bouncer—I knew what he was going to do and I managed to late cut it between gully and third slip. It would have gone for four but for some long grass and I had to settle for three, but he didn't try bouncing me again!

**Memorable stands and innings**

As far as I am aware the highest stand in a Sunday XI game was for 180 at **Widnes**. This was a partnership between Trevor Williams (Jack Williams' brother, who played for the MCC) and Phil Atherton. Trevor hit a century while Phil scored 80—there were no extras—before their wickets fell in quick succession.

I opened the batting with Ken Bold at **Appleton** and we shared a first-wicket partnership of 130, which was ended when I was out for 30. Ken went on to record his century—102 not out I think— I'm not sure how many sixes were in his innings but the ball visited neighbouring fields and gardens quite frequently.

Now the convention has been established that we retire at 50 the record is unlikely ever to be beaten, but there was one occasion when I was opening with Roger Pink at Toft—a beautiful place to play cricket on the outskirts of Knutsford. I think we were playing **Midland Bank** again. I reached my 50 just before he did and our partnership must have been more than 100. I was struggling a bit early on and decided that attack was the best strategy— I've never played a better off-drive than one that I perfectly timed and crashed into the fence at some speed. That absolutely destroyed the bowler's confidence and I found the going much easier after that! We won the game quite comfortably. Roger was a very good 1st team player and was captain between Jack Williams stepping down and the time I took over the captaincy.

In a match against **Upton**, Alex Storey scored 38 in 4.1 overs to win the match. He was caught on the boundary but from Upton's point of view the damage had been done!

Friendly cricket is a great environment in which young talent can be nurtured and developed. As a teenage opener Ben Edmundson (now 1st team captain) scored 124—including 15 fours and 2 sixes—against **Oldfield**. He also hit an unbeaten 110 away to **Upton** and 129 versus **Burton** (including 18 fours and 4 sixes). Playing senior cricket, even if only friendlies, can provide a useful opportunity for young players to build confidence and showcase their abilities. It was clear in Ben's case that Rainhill had a very special player.

## Memorable players

There are a number of players who have served the Sunday team with distinction down the years and these are seven who really stand out in my memory.

Scott Clegg has the distinction of winning the Bowler of the Season award more times than any other Sunday player. His off-spin has been outwitting opposition batters for well over a decade.

The redoubtable Chris O'Toole won the Best Batsman award in 2014. Chris was a man with a lot of shots, but not one of them was defensive! He only had one way of playing—and that was in a style I can only describe as flamboyant and adventurous. He didn't know what it meant to play himself in. In a match against **Alder** in 2013, on dreadful pitch that everyone else struggled to score on, Chris smashed a magnificent unbeaten 51, and would have surely scored more if he hadn't been forced to retire. Thanks to his efforts, Rainhill reached 166-8 and then bowled out Alder for 102 with only one of their players managing to get into double figures. When Chris was in form he was a force to be reckoned with. Sadly, Chris died after suffering a heart attack during a match in 2016, when he was playing for Whitefield. He was aged just 50. We will remember him at Rainhill for his ostentatious shots—he was the Kevin Pietersen of the Sunday team!

Chris had previously played rugby union for Orrell and Preston Grasshoppers. He was a great Sunday player because his view of cricket was that it was there to be enjoyed.

**Chris O'Toole**

Another player from this era, Tony Bullock, won the Player of the Year award in 2014. Tony was a great all-rounder, best typified by his performance in the win at **Prescot & Odyssey** during that year. Prescot reached 239-8 from 45 overs, with Tony taking 3-44. He then hit an unbeaten 53 as the Sunday team chased down the target for the loss of just one wicket. Tony had a bit of everything—he could bowl well, he scored 234 runs in that season and he was a brilliant fielder on the boundary.

Ben Edmundson, who I've already mentioned, scored 448 runs for us in 2011 averaging 89.6. He also took 23 wickets at an average of 7.9.

Jeff Fitzhenry won the Batting Award more times than any other Sunday player and he had a particularly good season in 2009, when he averaged 44 with the bat. Jeff was later 3rd team captain.

Asif Junaid, like Chris O'Toole, was not someone who dedicated much time to learning defensive shots. As far as I am aware he holds the record for the highest ever score for the Sunday team. In 2017 he hit an incredible 179, which included a huge six into one of the gardens at the bottom end of the field.

In the same season Ben Smith, another talented batsman who only wished to play friendly cricket, scored 119. Both of these scores were in games in which the opposition did not wish to retire batters on reaching 50.

Over the years several players have gone the extra mile for the sake of the team; recently Richard Appleton supplemented his reliable opening batting with keeping wicket as there was no-one else to do it. Several years ago, another player joined the Sunday team and not only had he never played cricket before it's fair to say he didn't have much talent for either batting or bowling—and his fielding was worse! His first season was a struggle for him, but he persisted. In his second season he hit a fantastic cover drive and the boundary was the highlight of his season—and perhaps also his cricketing career! He's no longer with the club but he always gave 100 percent and he proved that enjoying Sunday cricket does not necessary involve scoring a lot of runs or taking wickets.

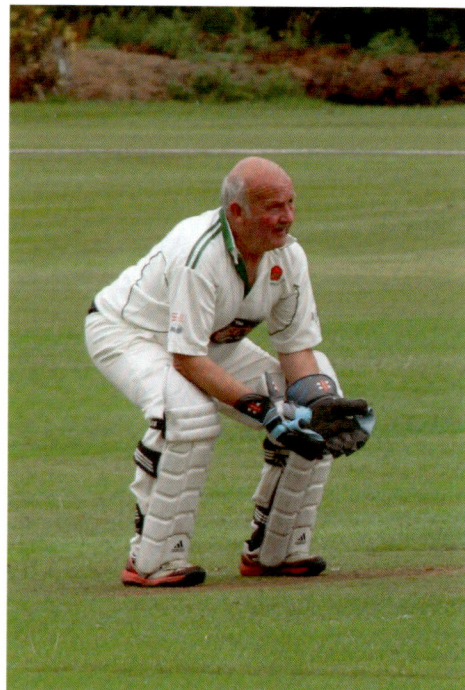

**Richard Appleton**

Cricket's a funny old game and Sunday cricket more so than other forms. In the only game we ever played at **Denbigh**, against the backdrop of Clwydian mountains, we began badly. Opening bowler Danny Sherratt bowled a beauty of a first ball that was dropped at point—the batsman went on to score a century! Danny continued to bowl economically and took two wickets, but the other bowlers suffered badly. The villagers brought up 200 without further loss at which point, with nothing to lose, I persuaded my reluctant son David to have a bowl. He completely bamboozled the centurion, and three other top/middle order batsmen, with his natural, completely untaught, leg cutters. David ended with 4-18, a phenomenal achievement, but the home side were on 250-6 at tea.

Knowing we lacked the firepower to chase down such a score, we opted for the next best thing—a draw. Andrew Dickenson, our reliable number 1 bat, was instructed to stay in for as long as possible. I told him, "never mind scoring, just stay in!" Geoff Boycott, then in his prime, could not have done better! He batted for over two and a half hours, to finish unbeaten at the close of play on 27 not out. He was supported by me, batting for 45 minutes, and then magnificently by David for an hour and a half. Heroics can come from unexpected sources and this was one match in which David excelled in all departments. We did hold out for the draw, which is perhaps—for the Sunday recreational cricketer at least—the best result of all.

There was a repeat performance—or a comparable one at least—at **Styal** when a very young Jack Lowrie, given similar instructions, batted throughout 40 overs to end not out in the 20s. He was partnered for the last 18 overs by Daniel Ball, who scored 1 not out to draw the game. Chris Tavaré would have been proud!  It was great to have Jack playing for us and I am sure he learned a lot as a young teenager given the opportunity to play Sunday cricket with senior players.

The Sunday XI isn't only about development, however—it's open to anyone. Simon Brown, 1st team wicketkeeper, played for the Sunday team in 2011 at Bury and scored an unbeaten 104. We don't see too many centuries now because of the convention of retiring at 50, but retiring batters can and do come back to the crease if all other wickets have fallen.

Similarly, because the nature of friendly cricket aims to ensure everyone who wants to gets to bowl, bowlers don't bowl long spells. This means they're less likely to come away with five-wicket hauls, but it does happen as Tony Bullock showed against **The Ashes** when he took 5-9 in 4 overs! Tony also took five wickets at **Upton**, but he needed 13 overs to achieve the feat on that occasion. Another memorable bowling performance was from Chris Partington away to **Worsley**, where he took 5-35 from 12 overs.

Anything can happen in Sunday friendlies and often does. Recreational cricket is many things, but it is never predictable. For example, in a drawn match against Frodsham in 2009 extras provided the highest score for both teams: Frodsham's 214-9 included 32 extras while Rainhill's extras column accounted for 41 runs in a total of 175-6! We usually have good games against Frodsham!

These are just a few personal highlights from 45 years with the Sunday XI. Hopefully there will be many more years to come. Rainhill Cricket Club has an ethos of providing cricket for all, and the Sunday team—rebranded as Rainhill Recreationals from 2022 onwards—is integral to achieving this.

*Joe Crossley is the captain of Rainhill Recreationals and Rainhill CC's longest serving player.*

**The annual match at Frodsham is often eventful**

# THE SUPPORTERS' TALE

**Supporters at the home match versus Leigh, 27.6.21**

A cricket club isn't a cricket club without supporters, which is why it would be remiss to tell the story of Rainhill's 150th anniversary season without taking into account their views.

Supporting a cricket club can be a vastly rewarding experience: there can be fewer better ways to enjoy a warm, sunny Saturday or Sunday afternoon than watching cricket. Cricket is, after all, a game that brings people together and united communities. Rainhill may be famous for the railway and Stephenson's *Rocket*, but in the minds of many of us it is our sports clubs that are the heartbeat of our community. The village without the cricket club would be unthinkable.

People support the cricket club for all kinds of reasons. Some are former players. Some are local businesses who recognise the value of the club to the community and take out sponsorships of various kinds—the club was particularly grateful to the ongoing support of several businesses which, during the Covid-19 pandemic, continued or increased their financial support during an uncertain time. Other supporters may be family members of players, parents of juniors or simply local people who enjoy an absorbing contest between cork and willow.

At a time when cricket has become more about spectacle and the big events (think T20 and "The Hundred") it is heartening that so many continue to support local cricket. As is the case with most other clubs, supporting Rainhill can be a frustrating business—you're as likely to be frustrated by the dramatic batting collapses and dropped catches as you are to be impressed by the scintillating strokeplay and superb bowling on display. But that's the nature of club cricket and our supporters wouldn't change it for anything.

Alan and Hilary Clarke have been supporting Rainhill for several seasons, and 2021 was a particular special one for them. Hilary explains: "What a year for us as spectator parents to proudly watch two brothers David Atkinson and James Clarke play in the first team together. With eight years between them, we would never have imagined they would both play in the same team. What an honour.

"We have thoroughly enjoyed being part of the Rainhill CC community and of course Alan has graduated to head barbecue chef too!" Typical of many supporters, Alan has willingly volunteered himself for various tasks including manning the barbecue at club events.

Another longstanding supporter is Victoria Ashcroft. The club has always played a big part in her life, not least as her father is Peter Mercer: "Rainhill CC has always been a huge part of our family with generations of great cricketers", she says.

"As a child, my sister and I would be taken to the home and away games when my Dad was playing. It wasn't just the cricket that we enjoyed, we loved playing with all the other children and running round the field when the games had finished! My mum also used to make the teas!

**The brothers celebrate a wicket**

"I have now grown up with two little girls of my own, one of which plays cricket for the under 9s and under 12s. To see my daughter be coached and have skills passed on to her by her grandad is very special to me. Rainhill CC will always hold a special place in our hearts."

Reflecting on the 150th anniversary season another supporter, Alan Higham, had this to say: "Last season epitomised so much of what Rainhill CC is about - community. Celebrations went beyond the immediate 'club family'. Rainhill CC is a community asset that is 150 years old and thriving, for good reasons.

"I will be forever grateful to the game of cricket in general, and Rainhill CC in particular, for the values they have helped to instil in my son as a teenager—and now as a young man in his twenties. I can never repay that debt in full, but as a Club Sponsor I can at least do something that helps future generations with their lives, in a fun and enjoyable way, through the truly 'beautiful game'."

Some parents become supporters when their children take up cricket and end up becoming involved in the broader life of the club. One such supporter is Craig Brougham. He says: "My family's involvement with the club came about entirely by chance and has grown to become a defining part of our lives and our children's childhoods. Attending one of the regular summer camps about 6 years ago led to both our sons joining the club and being involved in all levels of junior cricket. It has leached into our family business so much that even our 10-year-old daughter with her all-consuming gymnastics schedule has wanted to find time to squeeze in cricket matches when time allows.

"Cricket is a sport for the individual and for the team player. It occupies a curious space which both embraces exceptionalism (we can all see the individual talent on display from some very promising young players) whilst also championing team ethics and sporting collectivism. That's what makes it an ideal environment for a lot of Rainhill's young sports stars."

"My sons didn't really enjoy the slightly intimidating atmosphere of football when they were younger", explains Craig. "Individual brilliance is often baked-in to the status and success mentality of the game. In cricket they found a sport where different young people of different shapes, sizes and abilities could contribute to a team performance they could be proud of, whatever the result. Yes, they want to win, but they have been able to grow together as young people, have a laugh and celebrate victories either perilously tight or enjoyably large, and losses sometimes so catastrophic they have entered into legendary status amongst them and their peers.

**Craig Brougham**

"What matters is the camaraderie they have built between them having trained and played together for a number of years. That shapes childhoods. It builds memories and offers a safe space for the development of resilience and the robustness needed when tackling some of life's wider challenges."

Having become a supporter through his children's involvement at the club, Craig uses his time to volunteer in various ways. "It has been a privilege to regularly score for some of the junior teams and also to pen the junior match reports that have been gracing the website over the last few years. Finding interesting angles to approach the match reports has been a relatively easy task – these are very talented young players and their personalities, characters and teamplay have always made writing about them a real joy.

"I know how important it is for young people to read about themselves, to be seen and recognised for their efforts. I remember the buzz of reading my own name in a school magazine when I was a kid and for our young players it is important that their performances are recognised by the club alongside those of the adult league teams. I hope they have been similarly affected or had a little confidence-boost by reading about themselves. The greatest compliment I have been paid is a parent asking for a written copy of the match report I wrote when their son completed a famous hat-trick during an u13 game, as they wanted to keep it to read out during his 21st birthday celebrations. What a wonderful distillation of what Rainhill Cricket Club can do and can mean for the people of our community.

"My sons are getting older and we may get to a point when cricket is no longer part of their lives, but whether they continue to be part of the Club or not it remains a fantastic resource for Rainhill and it is wonderful seeing the Club so busy on a Friday evening during Junior nets, the ground buzzing with young voices and parents catching up and socialising while the next tranche of cricket superstars continue their development.  Long may it continue."

# THE GALA

Rainhill Cricket Club's Anniversary Gala took place on the Sunday of the August bank holiday weekend and was a fantastic success.

Celebrating 150 years since Rainhill Cricket Club was initially founded in 1871, the Gala was intended as a way of not only marking the anniversary but also reinforcing the club's role at the heart of the local community.

During the Gala under 9s coach John Pearson - with help from Alex Lea, Oliver Powell and Ken Rustidge - held fun coaching sessions for young people providing a taste of what the club regularly provides. Several new players signed up, and everyone involved enjoyed what was on offer - especially caterpillar cricket! Among the stallholders were representatives of local charities and businesses and there were various games on offer, some cricket related and some definitely not (including a giant, inflatable version of Twister). A face painter proved incredibly popular among younger attendees. The undoubted highlight of the afternoon was a rendition of Sweet Caroline, led by vocalist extraordinaire Mike Rotheram.

While the fantastic weather certainly helped, the number of people attending was still impressive. Several hundred people attended over the course of the day. Some were attending the club for the first time.

During the afternoon club captain Mike Rotheram was interviewed by Rainhill Rocks. He said: "This is a great attendance and I can't thank everyone enough - especially Rainhill Rocks for getting the word out. We've put on the gala a little bit to celebrate our 150th anniversary and a little bit to let the community know we're here... it's really about engaging the community. We provide for everyone, be it young children aged 5 and upwards, girls' cricket, boys' cricket, anyone who wants to play high standard cricket all the way through to recreational cricket. I'll be honest, we're also looking to raise money. We need a new scorebox and that's going to cost £15,000. But the main thing is community."

After the event Mike reflected that "we are really grateful for the support of Rainhill Community in making our gala a great success. Hundreds of families enjoyed the event which was helped by fine weather, good music and a friendly atmosphere. Many thanks to all the support we received from local businesses and charities with a special thanks to our main Club sponsor the Blue Mango."

The fact that the Gala went ahead at all was in no small part due to the efforts, determination, boundless energy and organisational skills of Carlo Albanese and Graham Powell. Not only did they have the vision for the event, they were able to persuade others (especially local businesses) to get involved and stimulated interest in the local area. It was a monumental effort from Carlo and Graham but one that was well worth it. The event not only raised over £2,400 but helped the club connect with the local community in a very positive way.

**Ryan Meah, club sponsor and owner of the Blue Mango restaurant**

There were many other volunteers who took part, from preparing food to tidying up the ground afterwards. First team captain Ben Edmundson, who spent the day manning the barbecue with Alan Clarke and fellow players Liam O'Toole and Stuart Brown, said: "What a day… huge credit to Carlo and Graham for all their hard work! Without these two this event would have been a non-starter! One of the best days I have been involved in during my 19 years at the club! Hopefully this can be a sign of things to come!"

Graham Powell added his personal thanks to a number of people: "Mike's raconteur skills were superb in getting the energy going and spreading the name of Rainhill Cricket. Further thanks to

**Liam O'Toole and Stuart Brown manned the burger stall**

Ben, Alan and Liam for their stamina at the BBQ, to John Pearson for the children's enjoyment. Special thanks to Craig, Ryan and Andrew. We must recognise the important help provided by the younger players and parents alike. Final thanks to the ladies - Gayle, Susan, Andrea, Sue, Lindsey and many others not listed."

The Gala certainly had the "feel good factor" and was so successful that the club plans to make it an annual event. Something intended to celebrate our history has become an important part of our future!

# Photos from the RCC 150th Anniversary Gala

Mike Rotheram entertains the crowd

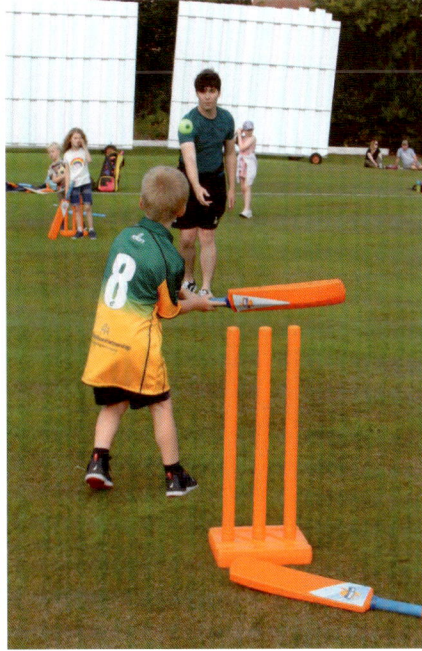

Oliver Powell shows how it's done

Some of the visitors were quite scary

Children enjoyed face painting...

...while everyone else enjoyed the weather.

Andrew Page ran a memorabilia stall

The bouncy castles were very popular

**John Pearson oversaw some fun skills workshops for children**

**Ollie, Ken, John and Alex with the young cricketers**

# ANNUAL AWARDS

Rainhill Cricket Club's annual awards event took place on Sunday 10th October 2021 at the Blue Mango restaurant—a longstanding sponsor of the club. Junior prizes were presented by England batsman Keaton Jennings.

The winners of the awards were as follows:

**Under 15s**
Most improved player: Ollie Unsworth
Batting award: Stevie Pennington
Bowling award: Sam Addy
Players' player of the year: Stevie Pennington and Sam Addy

**Under 13s**
Most improved player: Kieran Rose
Batting award: Stevie Pennington
Bowling award: Jack Tyms
Player of the year: Stevie Pennington

**Under 11s**
Most improved player: Finlay Venables
Batting award: Nathan Lawler
Bowling award: Finnlee Millar
Player of the year: Naithan Varghese and Mattie Ambage

**Under 9s**

Awards were presented to all under 9s who had played in a tournament

**Under 18s girls**

Most improved player: Paris Cook
Batting award: Sarah Curlett
Bowling award: Lucy Strettle
Players' player of the year: Katie Roberts

**Under 15s girls**
Batting award: Lily Murphy
Bowling award: Amber Bowie & Chloe Gillespie
Players' player of the year: Katie Roberts

**Under 10s girls**

The under 10s team completed the season with a 100% winning record: played 13, won 13. Consequently, all players were presented with a trophy commemorating the achievement.

**Womens' team**

Most improved player: Julie Foulkes
Batting award: Bobbie Grant
Bowling award: Susan Rotheram
Players' player of the year: Sue Lowrie

**Sunday XI**

Most improved player: Adam Lawler
Batting award: Vinny Varghese
Bowling award: Steve Bell
Players' player of the year (Joe Crossley Trophy): Paul Millar

**3rd XI**

Batting award: Neil Robinson
Bowling award: John Ball
Player of the year: Ethan Powell

**2nd XI**

Most improved player: Luis Duffy
Batting award: Mark Viggars
Bowling award: Sam Williamson
Player of the year: Ethan Powell

**1st XI**

Most improved player: Jack Lowrie
Batting award: Tyler McGladdery
Bowling award: Peter Kelly
Player of the year: Tyler McGladdery

## Club awards

Clubman of the year: John Pearson
Young player of the year: Jack Lowrie
Outstanding service: John Veacock and Tom McKeown
Chairman's award: Phil Morgan
President's award / Long Service Award: Andrew Finney

"We really want to thank John for all his effort this year. As a volunteer doing the treasurer's role, the coaching role and the umpiring it's been a fantastic effort. He's also going to sponsor a kit for the under 9s team and footed the bill for £300 to allow the girls to go to an under 9s tournament. John has also organised All-Stars and Dynamos. Added to that all the work he does on the treasury side, this award is very well deserved."

**CLUBMAN OF THE YEAR: John Pearson**          Peter Mercer

"We'd like to thank Andrew for his dedication and commitment over the years. I work out that he's scored in 1,500 games which is somewhere around 7-8,000 hours. He's entered over 500,000 runs into the scorebook and seen over 500 different players in the 1st team alone. He's scored in five different leagues and witnessed Rainhill winning five championships and seven cups. Honestly, we owe Andrew a huge debt of gratitude."

Peter Mercer

**PRESIDENT'S AWARD: Andrew Finney**

# Photos from the RCC Annual Awards Presentation

Jack Tyms

Nathan Lawler

Finnlee Millar

Sam Addy and Stevie Pennington

Alex Lea

Rainhill under-9s

Under-10s girls

Joe Crossley

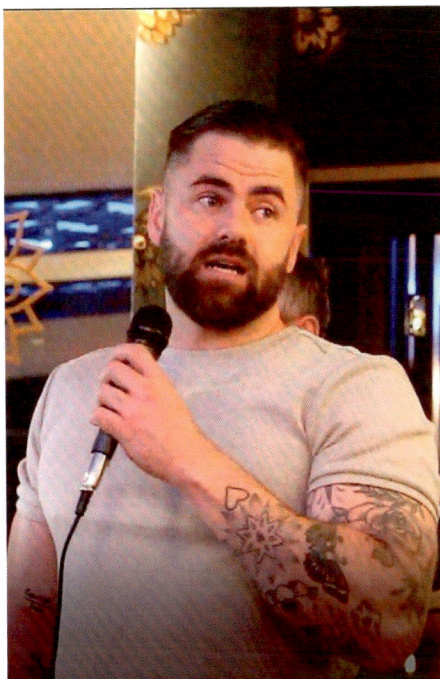

Jamie Harrison

Finlay Venables

Mattie Ambage

Xanthe Page

Heidi Page

Mike Rotheram

Peter Mercer

# TRIBUTES TO A CLUB LEGEND

**John Pearson**

John Pearson, to whom this book is dedicated, sadly passed away suddenly on 1st March 2022. His passing came as a great shock to everyone at Rainhill Cricket Club, as well as to the wider local cricketing community.

John served Rainhill CC in a variety of roles over many years. It is probably easier to list the roles he didn't have: he was a coach, a team manager, a committee member, club treasurer, and Activator for All-Stars and Dynamos.  He was also a well-respected umpire, known for his fairness and integrity—but principally for his love of cricket.

To describe John as a legend is not to do justice to the incredible contribution he has made to club and community. He was a driving force behind so many positive initiatives and his legacy is immense.  But it would be wrong to remember him only in terms of his contributions and what he has done for the club: John was also one of the great characters at Rainhill CC. His enthusiasm, zest for life, sense of humour and belief that cricket should be for everyone made him popular wherever he went.

In the aftermath of John's passing the club received many tributes, which we are publishing here alongside some photographs of John doing what he enjoyed most. The club believes that these tributes capture exactly the kind of person John was and show how much he meant to those who knew him, as well as how much the club meant to him.  Just two weeks before he passed away the club had nominated John to be a baton bearer for the Commonwealth Games baton relay, such was the esteem in which he was held.  He was a great man who will be fondly remembered.

"Absolutely devastating news. The club meant so much to John. Such a gentleman, kind, caring and always gave his time to other people. This kids and the parents absolutely adored him as did the seniors in the club. A true legend in every sense of the word. Such a kind man who absolutely loved the club, the parents and most importantly the juniors. He was the pied piper - he will be so badly missed. RIP John."
**Mike Rotheram, Club Captain**

"John was a true gentleman and invaluable member of our club. He had an unassuming friendly manner and his popularity was immense.

"John was a driving force with the development of Junior Cricket , undoubtedly an inspiration to our juniors and was highly regarded by parents. His commitment to the Club is highlighted by the roles he was taking on: Treasurer, Coach, All Stars/ Dynamos Activator, Umpire and Junior Team Manager. I will miss my own regular interaction on 'club matters' with him managing the clubs finances so effectively. I will always remember fondly and it was a pleasure to have been able to present John with the Clubman of the Year award at the October 21 presentation event and see the pride and joy the award gave him. His legacy at Rainhill CC will indeed be long lasting.

"John will be greatly missed by all and our condolences go to his family and friends."
**Peter Mercer, Club President**

" Very sad to lose such a popular man and a great servant to Rainhill CC.

"John covered so many important roles for the club in such a diligent and enthusiastic manner. He was friendly with everyone, but will be especially remembered for his impact with junior cricket and the high regard parents held him in.

"We will all greatly miss John as a friend and Club member of the highest standing.

"My deepest sympathies to John's family and friends."
**John Rotheram, Club Chairman**

"Such sad news about John. He was an amazing member of the Rainhill CC family. Emily loved having him as her coach and he will be sorely missed. Thoughts are with his family at this time."
**Vicci Ashcroft**

"I am totally lost for words and it will be a difficult time for the Club without John's enthusiasm, his zest and love for the game at all levels, and of course most importantly in the junior section."
**Craig Brougham**

"A genuine man who gave so much to others. He will be greatly missed by everyone at the club."
**Martin Lowrie**

"On a perfect summer's day at the Rainhill cricket club gala, in 2021, the opportunity for our 7 year old twin daughters came along to have their first real taste of cricket. Both nervous, they cued up in line to register for a special one hour session.

"They were greeted by a smiling, friendly face. The calm and reassuring nature of John Pearson

had them instantly relaxed and having fun, in no time. His soft and friendly voice was perfect for teaching children, the fundamentals of the game - always encouraging them without judgement and a unique ability to communicate with the most fragile age group.

"Only weeks later the girls had signed up to play for the under 9s. They were invited to a presentation day, where John's eyes were once again lit up by their presence. It was as if every child he coached was his own grandchild. He paid them so much attention and treated them with so much care and respect. John was constantly putting his own time and money into the team, it seemed as if youth cricket was everything he lived for.

"After coaching the girls through the winter indoor season and having many successful performances. The girls developed skills week by week and formed strong bonds with their team mates. On Friday the 25th of February, the girls attended another excellent training session and John was on top form as usual.

"We were all heartbroken by the news that came through, only a few days later, that John had sadly passed away. But with heavy hearts we are left with the blessed feeling that, although we only knew John for a short time, he has left us with a legacy and memories that will last a lifetime. Rest in peace John, you will be forever in our hearts."
**The Stokoe family**

"Lovely man and did so much for the club and the kids. Good night, God bless John. Love to his family and all who knew him. So, so sad."
**Gayle Albanese Jones**

"Clubs need the Johns of this world - people who get involved for the good of others. Some little All Stars player will grow up to become a great player and it all started with him. Thanks for all you did John."
**The Curlett Family.**

"All very sad here. John was a lovely man, who contributed so much. The kids loved him. My son was talking about the 'fun games' John would organise. Thoughts to the club and his family."
**Lisa Griffiths**

"I have many memories of John, but what struck me about him was how much he enjoyed everything he did. He was absolutely dedicated to cricket, and most importantly to youth cricket. He was in his element around young people; he loved them and they loved him. All grown-ups were children first, and John was one of these people who never forgot that.

"You couldn't be around John and not feel his passion for the game. But he was passionate about many other things too. Three years ago I organised a charity cricket match for CALM (the Campaign Against Living Miserably). John found out about it and immediately offered his services as umpire. He wouldn't hear about any payment. He just wanted to be part of something that was for a cause he cared about. That was so typical of John."
**Andrew Page**

"Great person and a true sportsman. He always had time to ask about everyone whether it be football or cricket. Very, very sad news."
**Andrew Morris**

"Desperately sad news. John was universally liked by everyone in our league, did every job going at Rainhill, and worked particularly tirelessly with the youngsters. Condolences to John's family and all at Rainhill."
**Liverpool and District Cricket Competition**

"Terrible, terrible news! John was a brilliant fella and someone we looked forward to spending Saturdays with. Condolences from us all at Sutton."
**Sutton St Helens CC**

"He was a great bloke. So sorry to hear. Condolences to his family and friends."
**Greg Harvey**

"Very sad news, such a nice bloke and put a lot of hours into the club. Condolences to his family and friends."
**Chris Chambers, Women & Girls Cricket Pathway Manager, Lancashire Cricket.**

"Such sad news, John was always a great help with U9s games, tournaments and fixtures. He's enthusiasm towards all clubs was fantastic, he will missed."
**Greg Pennington, Cricket Development Officer, Lancashire Cricket Foundation**

"One of the nicest fellas you could wish to meet and a good umpire as well. Condolences from everyone at Maghull CC."
**Paul McKenna, Maghull CC**

"We are saddened to learn of the sudden death of John Pearson from the Merseyside Cricket Umpires' Association and Rainhill Cricket Club. John was a well respected umpire and we send our condolences to his family and friends."
**Maghull CC**

"John gave me the chance to play in my first ever tournament. He was a very generous man who taught me a lot about cricket."
**Xanthe Page, age 9**

"Awful news, such a nice guy and a huge influence on Rainhill CC. RIP John."
**Phil Curran**

"What a great shame gentleman of the highest order. Humble and gentle man who would do anything for anyone. R.I.P John."
**Kev Wilson**

"John was my uncle and was a great man have fond memories of him when I was growing up. He was a very hard working man and his passing will have such a huge impact on everybody that knew him. R.I.P. John till we meet again X"
**Kevin Hughes**

"Goodnight, God bless John. It was a pleasure to of known you and call you our friend. You'll be missed so much. From all of us at The Holt."
**Denise Blundell**

"Lovely bloke and good umpire."
**Mark Wilkie, Caldy CC**

"So sorry to hear this sad news. He was a lovely man. My thoughts and condolences to his family and friends."
**Alan Atkinson**

"I didn't have much interest in cricket until I went to All-Stars at Rainhill Cricket Club. I went there quite nervous that my children's energetic nature may be too much for the coaches. The first

coach I met was John he reassured me that all were welcome. He made everyone feel welcome and had so much patience and energy. He also made ordinary children feel like they were cricket superstars. I wish there were more people like John - he will be greatly missed by me and my family".
**Anna Page**

## Key to league tables

Pl: Played,

w: Won   wd: Won by default   wcn: Opposition conceded

wc: Won by concession

l: Lost   ld: Lost by default   lcn: Team Conceded   lc: Lost by concession

d: Draw

t: Tied

Ab / a: Abandoned

ND: No decision

c: Cancelled

BatP: Batting Bonus Points   BowlP: Bowling Bonus Points

Pen: Penalty Points

Pts: Points

# INDEX

Numbers in **bold** refer to pages with illustrations